ON THE ROAD city
Milan

ON THE ROAD
Editor of collection
Laura Andreini

editorial project
Forma Edizioni srl, Firenze, Italia
redazione@formaedizioni.it
www.formaedizioni.it

editorial production
Archea Associati

editorial direction
Laura Andreini

author
Matteo Moscatelli

editorial staff
Valentina Muscedra
Maria Giulia Caliri

graphic design
Elisa Balducci
Alberto Bolzonetti
Vitoria Muzi
Isabella Peruzzi
Mauro Sampaolesi

translations
Katy Hannan

photolithography
Art and Pixel srl, Florence

printing
Gutenberg Press Limited,
Gudja Road, Tarxien, Malta PLA 19

texts by
Laura Andreini
Maria Grazia Folli
Matteo Moscatelli
Lorenzo Spagnoli
Giacomo Albo [41-65]
Daniele Bonzagni [52-67]
Giulia Canavotto [46]
Narghes Doust [42-72]
Michela Fumagalli [59-73]
Francesco Menegatti [24-80]
Stefano Moscatelli [12-17]
Lucia Paci [37]
Mario Redaelli [43-53]
Michele Roda [32-35]
Eleonora Salsa [23-44]
Eugenia Silvestri [82]

we would like to thank
Giacomo Albo
Marco Introini
Paola Ricas
Maddalena Tibertelli de Pisis
for their collaboration

New Edition: April 2017

ISBN 978-88-99534-25-7

Table of contents

Guidebook as tool

On the Road is a new collection of contemporary architecture guidebooks whose purpose is to tell about a place, whether a city or larger area, through its architectural works chosen to be visited and experienced directly.

Each guidebook comes in two versions. One is a convenient, pocket-sized printed version, and one is a digital version as an iPad app with extra images and information with an interactive satellite map including customized routes.

Likewise, the handy traditional version has a convenient special jacket that opens into a map marking the location of the architectural works and interesting sites to visit. On the back are miniature images and addresses of the architectural works described in detail within.

The book starts with short essays explaining the city or area's present day and history and outlining possible future scenarios with planned or imminent projects. The buildings are chosen from recent construction periods and are grouped to fit routes that can be visited in a single day. Each work features of a photograph of the whole, an architectural drawing (plan or section), a short description, and facts including architect, type, year of construction, address, website, and how to visit it.

The finest architecture of each city and suggested routes are represented by this collection of not-to-be-missed, "timeless" buildings that uniquely define their settings. General information and useful tips for travelers help them optimize their visits and quickly understand the essence of the place described.

Museums, theatres, restaurants, hotels and a list of top architectural firms working in the city let visitors turn a regular trip into an opportunity for study or work.

Milan

Laura Andreini*

Milan is the first Italian city to be included in the On the Road travel guide collection. Milan has been a city that has shown creativity and inspired strong interest in the modern and contemporary architecture that has been constructed and is currently under completion. In recent years, Milan has become a metropolis involved in transformations that are well worthy of interest for the architectural and urbanistic experiments that have been carried out. On one hand, Milan, as a whole, is an observatory of current living conditions and the problems involved, and on the other, it is itself the subject of observation, analysis and research.

Witness to the strong reflection currently focussed on Milan, was the section dedicated to the city in the Italian Pavilion curated by Cino Zucchi on the occasion of the 14th Venice Architectural Biennale. Milan will be observed from the viewpoint of its "anomalous modernity", a modernity that is typically Italian. The city becomes the emblem of a certain Italian idiosyncrasy, able to innovate and at the same time interpret the previous status of a past that it is impossible not to consider. An important example: the maestri of rationalism who adopted this attitude in their work and who had such a strong influence on the architectural evolution of the city. Their influence can also be seen in the most recent architectural projects, and for this reason, certain fundamental buildings of the Milan Rationalist School will be included in the guide.

The complex dialectics between innovation and respect for the existing urban form is the distinctive characteristic of Milan: recovery of downgraded neighbourhoods, redevelopment of decommissioned industrial zones, technological experimentation, and vertical development are the aspects that mark Milan as a strongly contemporary city. This guide is being launched in answer to a moment of great focus on Milan. As it guides the reader through the wide range of contemporary architectural projects, it emphasises the unique nature of its complex character. The transformations are still underway and for this reason, it is difficult to foresee how a city of such size will manage to redefine its personal equilibrium: but this too is part of the contemporary nature of Milan.

* Architect and Associate Professor. Teaches and researches at the DIDA of Florence and works at Studio Archea of which she is co-founder; writer and Deputy Editor-in-Chief for *Area* magazine.

Political / geographical facts

country
Italy

language
italian

area code
+39 02

coordinates
45 28' 38" N
9° 10' 53" E

area
181,67 sq. km

population
1,336,364

density
7,356 inhabitants / sq.km

time zone
UTC+1

city website
www.comune.milano.it

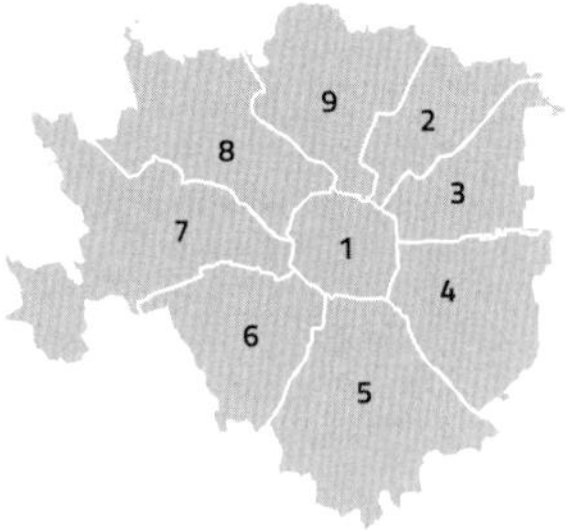

Administrative districts

1. Milan City Centre
2. Central Station, Gorla, Turro, Greco, Crescenzago
3. Città Studi, Lambrate, Venezia
4. Vittoria, Forlanini
5. Vigentino, Chiaravalle, Gratosoglio
6. Barona, Lorenteggio
7. Baggio, De Angeli, San Siro
8. Fiera, Gallaratese, San Leonardo, Quarto Oggiaro
9. Garibaldi Station, Niguarda

General information
useful addresses and numbers

INFORMATION OFFICES

InfoMilano Tourist Office
Galleria Vittorio Emanuele -
corner of Piazza della Scala
+39 02 88455555
Mon – Fri / 9 am – 7 pm
Sat / 9 am – 6 pm
Sun. and holidays / 10 am – 6pm
25 Dec, 1 Jan, 1 May / closed

Central Station Info counter
Departure hall – side track 21
+39 02 77404318 / 4319
Mon – Fri / 9 am – 5 pm
Sat, Sun, holidays / 9 am – 12 pm
25 Dec, 1 Jan, 1 May / closed

Fondazione Riccardo Catella (Porta Nuova area Infopoint)
Via Gaetano De Castillia, 28
+39 02 45475195 / 96
Mon – Fri / 12.30 pm – 2.30 pm
Sat / 10 am – 1 pm and 2 pm – 5 pm

EMERGENCY SERVICES

Carabinieri 112
Police 113
Emergency medical service 118
Fire Department 115
24-hour Pharmacy 800 801185

URBAN TRANSPORT*

Bus and Tram
Tickets: can be bought from ATM Points, ATM Milano Official App, bars, news-stands and Tabacchi (cigarette) stores
www.atm.it

Subway (4 city lines)
Tickets: can be bought from ATM Points, ATM Milano Official App, bars, news-stands and Tabacchi (cigarette) stores
www.atm.it

Passante Railway (11 suburban lines)
Tickets: For urban sections: from bus, tram and subway sales points. For suburban sections, tickets from railway stations

Taxi
+39 02 6969; +39 02 4040; +39 02 6767

Bicycle rentals

BikeMi
Automatic bike rental with subscription (annual, weekly, or daily) from their website, via mobile website, at ATM Points or Infoline
www.bikemi.com

GENERAL CONSULATE OF CHINA
Via Benaco, 4 - 20139 Milan
+39 02 5694106

GENERAL CONSULATE OF FRANCE
Via della Moscova, 12 - 20121 Milan
+39 02 6559141

GENERAL CONSULATE OF GERMANY
Via Solferino, 40 - 20121 Milan
+39 02 6559141

GENERAL CONSULATE OF GREAT BRITAIN
Via San Paolo, 7 - 20121 Milan
+39 02 723001

GENERAL CONSULATE OF THE RUSSIAN FEDERATION
Via Sant'Aquilino, 3 - 20148 Milan
+39 02 723001

GENERAL CONSULATE OF THE UNITED STATES
Via Principe Amedeo 2/10 - 20121 Milan
+ 39 02 290351

HOW TO PHONE

From a local landline: dial the area code (02) and then the number

From a foreign landline: dial the international code (+39), area code (02) and the number

* Ticket categories: Urban tickets, Day pass, Two-day pass.
RicaricaMi Pass: Four different types of ticket can be recharged on this pass.
Rho Fiera Milano: A special ticket is required.
Air Bus: Shuttle bus service between Linate Airport and the Central Station.

Useful tips

1. Milan offers a large range of hotel choices according to the budget available. In the top quality category there are the famous historic hotels (like the **Grand Hotel et de Milan** or the **Hotel Excelsior Gallia**), or the more modern boutique hotels (like **Armani Hotel Milano** or **Hotel Boscolo Milano**). For medium to lower priced accommodation, not always in the city centre, it is advisable to choose according to the areas you wish to visit. For even more economic solutions, the best alternative is to stay at one of the many hostels or B&Bs in the city centre.

2. Single tickets (Biglietti Urbani), one-day tickets (Biglietti Giornalieri) or two-day tickets (Bigiornalieri) can be bought for **public transport** travel around the city. The electronic RicaricaMi system allows you to charge four different types of ticket on the pass. A day-ticket is not sufficient to reach the Rho Fair Grounds, so you will need to buy a specific ticket for that destination. All the locations described in the guide can be accessed by public transport, but in certain cases (such as the two Greater Milan tours); it is advisable to check the timetable and any changes in route very carefully.

3. Another system for moving around Milan is with **Car Sharing or Bike Sharing**. There are several options for **Car Sharing** such as GuidaMi (ATM), Car2go (Daimler), Enjoy (ENI with Fiat and Trenitalia) or E-vai (Trenord and Sems), that vary according to the type of vehicle and availability, parking systems and access to preferential traffic lanes. BikeMi offers a **Bike Sharing** service, available with a daily, weekly or yearly subscription: the maximum bike use is two hours each time, but the first half-hour is free.

4. There are several places where visitors can enjoy a panoramic view of the city, especially in the centre. Some are easily accessible (with an entry ticket) like the **roof of the Duomo** (Cathedral) or from the **Torre Branca** (Viale Alemagna) designed by Gio Ponti and Cesare Chiodi. Others are the terraces of restaurants and cocktail bars like the Terrazza Martini (Piazza Diaz 7), Terrazza Aperol (Piazza del Duomo), Terrazza 12 (Via Durini 28), Ceresio 7 (Via Ceresio 7), Brera Garden Floor (Via dell'Orso 7), La Terrazza di Via Palestro (Via Palestro 2) and the Globe (Piazza V Giornate 1).

5. Other panoramic views can be seen from the tall office blocks in the city centre. It is possible to visit certain building inside, like the **Pirelli Skyscraper/25**, **Palazzo Lombardia/28** or **Unicredit Headquarters/31,** although only on established days and times: It is advisable to enquire about available times and any possible booking requirements.

6. For greater information about the transformations underway in Milan, the **Urban Centre** is the reference point that can supply a range of updated information. The centre is located in the Galleria Vittorio Emanuele; during the year, there are exhibitions, conferences and meetings open to the public on subjects closely linked with the development of the city.

7. For an overall panorama of the **Porta Nuova Garibaldi-Varesine-Isola project /28-35**, it is worth visiting the Fondazione Riccardo Catella (Via de Castillia 28). The building hosts an exhibition showing all the general features of the intervention and information concerning all the main projects; the exhibition presents images, video films and a model of the master plan. The Foundation also promotes meetings and debates on subjects linked with sustainable development of the territory and urban quality improvements.

8. Choosing the best moment to visit Milan depends on different factors. As far as weather is concerned, the period between March and October is the most comfortable: the city is half-deserted in August, but temperatures can sometimes be very hot. Another aspect to consider are the events held throughout the year. It is useful to obtain a calendar of the exhibitions, the theatre season program, as well as the events organised at the Milan Fair. In April is the famous furniture and design fair, the **Salone del Mobile**, one of the most important furnishing sector meetings in the world. During the period of the fair, Milan also holds the **Fuorisalone**, with fashion and design events, exhibitions, performances, and presentations in various areas of the city centre.

9. Milan is a **river city** and, even though parts of the canal system have been buried, it is still possible to enjoy many of the remaining Milan canals. The Naviglio della Martesana (northeast), the Naviglio Grande and the Naviglio Pavese (southwest) are not only an important part of Milan's historical past, but are also a departure point for pleasant tours. Visitors can ride bikes along cycling paths through green countryside, or take a cruise on one of the canal boats to visit the outskirts of the city.

The most significant stages of urban structure in Milan

Lorenzo Spagnoli*

In the history of Milan, it is possible to identify certain passages that, alongside the economic and social transformations, demonstrate the changes in the structural concept of the city and the territory in general. In the late Middle Ages, the first overall images of the city – which had expanded gradually in concentric circles around the ancient Roman nucleus within the city walls– provided a religious and cosmic interpretation, but with the arrival of Renaissance culture, there was a radical change in the concept of urban structure.

In the 15th century, the problematic relationship between architecture and urban structure became obvious. In fact, architectural projects like the Ospedale Maggiore by Filarete, under construction since 1460, proposed a rational urban layout that was proving difficult to achieve, as became evident a few decades later with the urban planning designed by Leonardo da Vinci. Working in Milan from 1482, Leonardo considered the city fabric too densely constructed and drew up sketches of his ideal city, but which was certainly based on Milan and Lombardy, in which beauty was not distinct from the use of techniques that would provide a high standard of living for the middle classes and, at the same time, would eliminate the "infinite evils" that marked the areas inhabited by the poorer classes. However, his concepts and projects, like those for reforming the suburban area of Porta Vercellina in 1497-1498, did not lead to any discernible practical results. Even during the course of the 16th century, decisive changes in urban functionality were developed only in relation to essential military needs; there was no outcome for projects like that proposed by the Genovese banker Tommaso de' Marini, who wanted to connect Piazza Mercanti with his residence in Palazzo Marino with a "new road", two hundred metres long. The comparison between Francesco Richini's map of 1603 and that of Marc'Antonio del Re (1734) drawn up during the Austrian domination, revealed that even in the 17th century, any transformations made to the Milanese urban structure were relatively small. Even important architectural projects in the latter half of the century – including the Teatro alla Scala by Piermarini – indicate that public spaces may have been significant but were still quite limited. Even in the impressive Italy conquered by Napoleon in 1796, the imposing project by Giovanni Antolini for the Foro Bonaparte in 1801, in the plans drawn the same year by Pinchetti, did not show any significant impact on the consolidated urban fabric.

It was only in 1807 that a new stage for opening up the city within the Spanish walls seemed to be taken into consideration with a plan drawn up in 1807 by the Ornato Commission that proposed the construction of a series of straight roads, including Corso Napoleone, which would have connected the Castello with the Ospedale Maggiore. This plan was also abandoned, but in the early years after the Unification of Italy the pressure placed on the old tissue of the central areas was increased; the cruciform Galleria Vittorio Emanuele, under construction since 1864, created a link between Piazza Duomo and the Piazza della Scala. However, it was only in 1884, that it was decided to draw up a plan that was able to define a global picture for the development of a city that by now had a population of over 300,000 inhabitants. The plan by the municipal engineer Beruto, adopted in 1889, was the first of a series of grid layouts; it provided for the opening up of certain streets within the consolidated urban centre and, outside this area, a network connected by a regular series of piazzas. The same urban plan was used as a base for the following plans created in 1912 and 1934 through which, with increasing difficulty, attempts were made to contain the precipitous urban expansion within a repetitive geometrical layout of further roads.

At the end of the Second World War, with the AR plan by the Milanese rational architects (1944-1945) a new stage began, focussing strong attention on the regional aspect. The attempt to make predictions concerning the metropolitan area was proposed again in 1959 with the creation of the PIM (Milanese Intercommunal Plan) with a series of strategic documents on successive territorial scales, and with the Documento di inquadramento of 2000 that connected the various distribution pattern dynamics, especially in service industry sectors, with a flow based in two main directions, one of which ran from east to west between the two airports of Malpensa and Linate.

Lastly, the recent development of a city indicated as one of the nodes of global economy has occurred in a dual urban and territorial perspective. In an era when the flow of financial capital is at a maximum, "global real estate" operations have led to radical changes in many areas that have been undeveloped or decommissioned for many years (we need only mention the large redevelopment project concerning the area running from the Garibaldi Station to Piazza della Repubblica, and from Porta Nuova to Palazzo Lombardia) in the traditional outskirts of greater Milan well outside the communal borders. However, there are also parts of the city and the hinterland where the evident signs of hardship require a new stage of strong political, economic, social and urbanistic commitment.

* Former Professor of Architectural and Urban Design and History of Urban Planning at the Faculty of Architecture at the Politecnico University of Milan.

Twentieth century architecture in Milan

Maria Grazia Folli*

Milan was the major industrial city in Italy during the country's post-unification period and for decades during the last century the city underwent an intense program of building construction that allowed it to play an important role in the modernisation of Italy's architecture. Already back in 1923, only a few years after the end of the First World War, the composition and constructive solutions adopted for Cà Brütta by Giovanni Muzio in via Moscova expressed the desire to go beyond the neo-eclectic return to the late Arte Nouveau style of the Liberty period. In a return to a sober neo-classical model and metaphysical atmosphere Muzio's design helped foster a new movement in the 20th century that was aimed at countering the unruliness of the Futuristic Avant Garde with project proposals based on "classical" urbanity values. Adepts who adhered to the new direction were Milanese architects such as Giuseppe De Finetti (Casa della Meridiana, 1925); Aldo Andreani (Palazzo Fidia, 1930); Piero Portaluppi (Planetario, 1930); Emilio Lancia (Torre Rasini, in collaboration with Gio Ponti, 1934), who promoted diversified interpretations of the poetics introduced in Cà Brütta. In fact, Gio Ponti, who initially based his work on common 20th century models (Building in via Domenichino, 1930), seemed more interested than other architects in gradually relinquishing the neoclassical direction in favour of German or French architectural culture, as is evident in his constructive and distributive language for the Montecatini Complex (1938).

Moreover, back in 1926 a group of young designers from the architectural school of the Politecnico University of Milan set up the Gruppo 7 basing their theories on the paradigms of international rationalism that was considered more suitable to represent the transformation of building construction in a modern version. One of the members of the group was the most important Italian modernist architect, Giuseppe Terragni, from Como, designer of the ex Casa del Fascio in Como (1936) and famous in Milan for the controversial concept of his Casa Rustici housing complex (1936). Other members who joined Gruppo 7 were Luigi Figini (Villa Figini, 1935) and Gino Pollini (multi-storey town houses) in collaboration with Figini, 1934) who carried out experiments on rational concepts later used by Mario Asnago and Claudio Vender (Habitation in viale Tunisia, 1936) in works that stand out for the refined blend of functional choices and subtle metaphysical references. The functionalist models served as inspiration above all for the various social housing projects built between 1930 and 1940 in the suburbs of Milan. Among the architects who worked on these projects were Franco Albini, Renato Camus, Giancarlo Palanti who designed the Fabio Filzi quarter (1938) and the Ettore Ponti quarter (1941).

At the end of the Second World War, reconstruction plans faced the need to reorganise the central and suburban areas; designs were based either on international modernity or relied on solutions inspired by recovering local historical references and pre-existing environments. The BBPR group composed of Gian Luigi Banfi, Lodovico Barbiano di Belgiojoso, Enrico Peressutti, and Ernesto Nathan Rogers based the inspiration for the restoration of the Castello Sforzesco and the configuration of the relative castle museums (1958) on a critical revision of the rationalist paradigms). But it was above all with the construction of the Torre Velasca (1958), also by BBPR, that the idea of the high-rise building was inspired by the 15th century tower built by Filarete, unlike the formal and constructive experimentation of the sky-scraper style by Luigi Mattioni (Terrazza Martini,1954); Melchiorre Bega (Torre Galfa 1959); Vico Magistretti and Franco Longoni (Apartment tower in park, 1956), and above all, Gio Ponti, designer of the famous Pirelli Tower (in collaboration with Fornaroli, Rosselli, Valtolina, Dell'Orto, Danusso, Nervi, 1960). In the same way subtle references to the past can be seen in the buildings by Ignazio Gardella (INA Residential neighbourhoods in Cesate, in collaboration with Albini, 1952) or by Luigi Caccia Dominioni (Casa Caccia Dominioni, 1950); these are in contrast with the "modernity" of Vittoriano Viganò (Istituto Marchiondi, 1957), Angelo Mangiarotti and Bruno Morassutti (Residential home in via Quadronno, 1960); Franco Albini and Franca Helg (organisation of the Milanese underground rail system 1964); and above all the transgressively original architecture of Luigi Moretti (in particular the Corso Italia complex, 1955).

Milan consolidated its role during the years of the economic boom with renewed interest in the suburban areas where many interventions were carried out, conceived as micro urban areas: the Monte Amiata complex (1974) by Carlo Aymonino, the housing complex in the Gallaratese quarter by Aldo Rossi (1973), and the university buildings and residential units in the Bicocca quarter (1998) by Vittorio Gregotti. At the same time, there was a new interest in building office space on the outskirts of Milan, such as the Mondadori headquarters at Segrate (1975) designed by Oscar Niemeyer; the fifth ENI office building at San Donato Milanese (1991) by Roberto Gabetti and Aimaro Isola (1991) and the main offices of the Sole 24 Ore newspaper in Milan (2004) by Renzo Piano, all of which were works representative of a post-modernity in search of disenchanted images far from any ideological aspiration.

* Full Professor at Politecnico University of Milan.

Milan 2000-2015, a changing skyline, urban renewal and evolving forms of habitation

Matteo Moscatelli*

Unlike the 1990s, which was marked by a period of stagnation caused by several factors (beginning with the judicial events of 1992) the last fifteen years have represented a turning point in Milan thanks to widespread transformations that have involved areas with a range of different problems (city centre, consolidated city, suburbs) and multiple aspects (empty spaces, urban blocks, districts). Although it is not easy to provide a conclusive picture of the changes because of the diversity of type and application and because many projects are still underway, it is possible to recognise certain recurring themes that have formed the basis for the proposed projects.

The first and most immediately noticeable aspect that is even more evident when viewing Milan from high-lying points in the surrounding region is the change in the urban skyline; the iconic buildings that have dominated the urban profile for over sixty years (the Torre Velasca and Pirelli Tower above all) are now flanked and surpassed by new vertical buildings destined both for business (Torre Unicredit) and habitation (Torre Tirana), located in the city centre (Palazzo Lombardia) and in the suburbs (Torre RCS). Some are representative of the history and constructive traditions of the area (Edifici al Portello), as well as more general fields of research, not simply local (the Bosco Verticale), or limited to the "signatures" of their designers (City life).

The second aspect to be emphasised, not only because of the ground conservation policy that is aimed at giving precedence to brownfield redevelopment rather than new occupation of greenfield areas, but also the desire to recover certain strategic spaces, concerns the regenerating nature of certain projects whose interest mainly consists of the coexistence of multi-scalar environments. In fact, on one hand the city is undergoing a series of master plans on a huge scale, like those involving Bicocca, Portello, the ex-Fiera zone and the Garibaldi-Varesine-Isola area. On the other hand, especially in the city's historical centre, there has been an increase of works on a smaller scale on existing buildings, focussed on technological and functional redevelopment (La Serenissima), change of function (Excelsior concept store), change of function and extension (Bi-La Fabbrica del Gioco e delle Arti), or faithful reconstruction of original buildings that had been destroyed (Padiglione d'Arte Contemporanea).

A third aspect concerns the type of intervention under consideration, because, unlike the past, it seems that certain opportunities for experimentation are making a come-back, even in areas destined for culture and habitation. The launching of cultural projects has been sustained by the creation of new educational buildings (CDD Centro per disabili), buildings for social projects and associations (Incubatore dell'Arte), but above all for expanding exhibition space (Museo del Novecento, Gallerie d'Italia,

Museo delle Culture, and the newly-established Feltrinelli and Prada foundations) as well as the interventions for the redevelopment and integration of the theatres in Milan (including the Teatro alla Scala, Teatro degli Arcimboldi, Teatro Franco Parenti ,and the Teatro Nazionale). Research on habitation has become a question of increasing importance in light of the housing emergency caused by the loss of income by the weaker sectors of society, the increase in medium and long-term redundancy, the increase in the number of single parent families, and old and inadequate existing housing. Although this problem has been dealt with only in part, with a large amount of potential still to be developed, in recent years several housing scheme contests have been held and realised (such as Abitare a Milano 1 and 2, Housing in Via Cenni, Housing Contest) which have generated positive opportunities for debate and which have involved private and public participants (Municipal and Regional Authorities, real estate funding, associations, cooperatives, and business companies).

Although these examples demonstrate how the current urban situation is composed of widespread and diversified projects, it seems appropriate to add two further in-depth reflections on what has been achieved and what is underway.

The first reflection concerns the "possible" Milan and what the city could have become, composed of a well-documented file of alternative proposals for areas that concern areas from the ex-Fiera to the Expo 2015 zones, the Bicocca and Milanofiori areas, and a range of operations that have not been realised or have been suspended, such as the BEIC project in Porta Vittoria and the Santa Giulia district. These projects lead to reflection on old vicissitudes on one hand, and also because careful analysis of the reasons that led to the identification and hierarchisation of certain themes demonstrate how great the expectations and needs of the community and financial promoters were in relation to the transformation of the city.

The second reflection involves the Milan of the future and what the city will become. The size and location of areas like the railway stations, decommissioned military barracks, and the spaces used by Expo after its conclusion predict how future development will depend not only on the imminent operational start-up of projects that are currently work sites underway or near termination, but also the results of reflection on a range of urban voids whose strategic importance demands a far greater multi-scale view in future debates, and a constantly evolving and more farsighted vision.

* Architect and PhD. Teaches university courses at Politecnico University and IED Design in Milan.

Torre al Parco
Giuseppe Meazza Stadium
Piazzale Cadorna

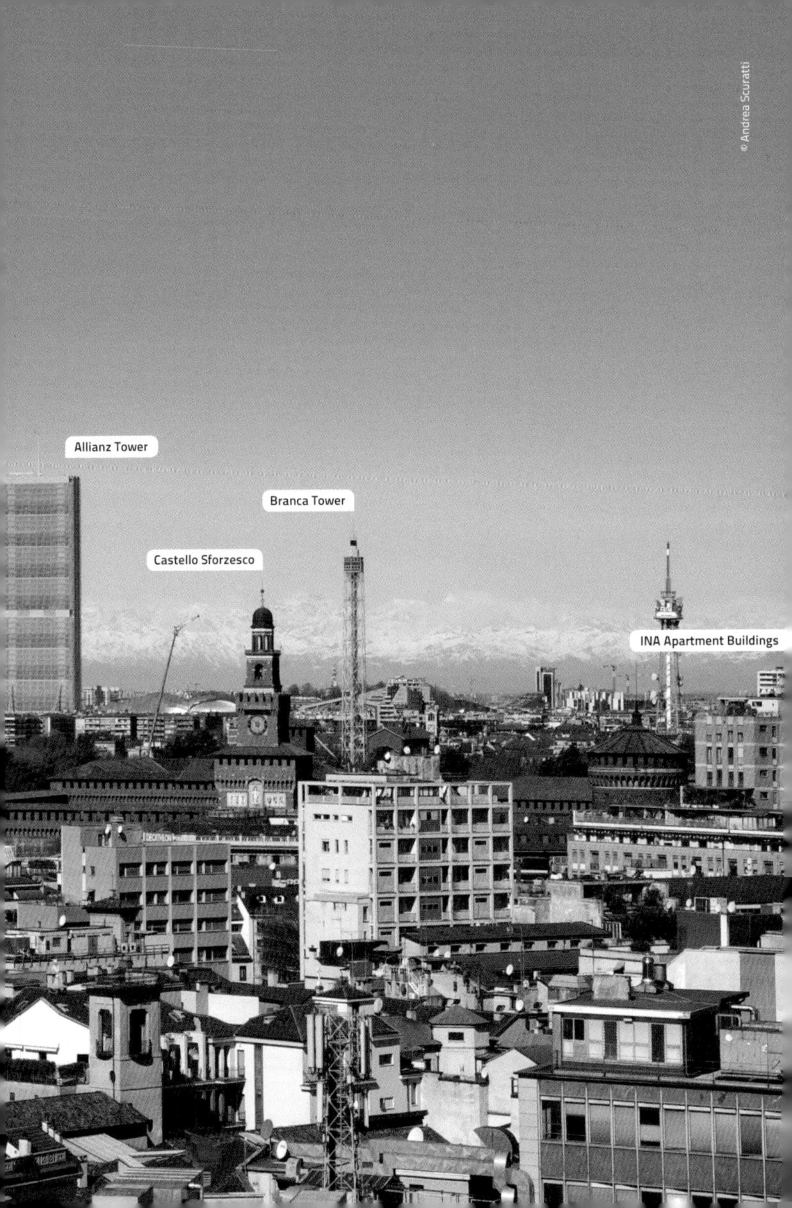
Allianz Tower
Branca Tower
Castello Sforzesco
INA Apartment Buildings
© Andrea Scuratti

Unicredit Headquarters
Solaria Tower
Bosco Verticale
Garibaldi Towers
Teatro alla Scala

Palazzo Lombardia
Diamond Tower
Breda Tower
The Pirelli Skyscraper
Galfa Tower
The Montecatini
Office Building
Gallerie d'Italia

Strategies for visiting Milan

It is better to count at least five or six days to visit Milan reasonably well. The places listed in the guide have been divided into five itineraries, each one needing a whole day. The tour of the centre includes buildings that can be visited internally, like some of the museums, and for this tour, it would be better to dedicate at least two days. The first two circuits can be followed almost entirely on foot, while public transport is needed for the last three tours.

Tour I - Milan City Centre
The original historical nucleus of Milan is Roman, and is composed of a dense compact urban fabric. The pedestrian area of the city centre begins with Piazza Duomo as far as Piazza San Babila along Corso Vittorio Emanuele as far as the Sforzesco Castle along Via Dante, down to Piazza della Scala and through the Galleria Vittorio Emanuele. This circuit is encircled by the traces of the old Spanish Walls and includes the main religious and civic monuments such as the **Duomo/13**, **Santa Maria delle Grazie/04**, **Ospedale Maggiore/08** and the **Sforzesco Castle/02**. This area contains some of the main cultural attractions including museums like the **Gallerie d'Italia/15** or the **Museo del Novecento/12**, and several theatres beginning with the **Teatro alla Scala/14**. Many of these buildings are like geological layers of the history of Milan since they have been subject to redevelopment, change of use and expansion that have modified the original character over time. Near the Piazza Duomo rise the **Velasca Tower/09** and the **Corso Italia Complex/10**, two of the most significant constructions of post-war Milan.

Tour II - Garibaldi - Repubblica - Porta Venezia
This circuit leads north and northeast from the city centre outside the line of the Spanish Walls, to enter the route of the Circonvallazione esterna ring road. The Porta Nuova Garibaldi-Isola-Varesine area is the location of one of the most important urban redevelopment schemes of recent years: this is the new skyscraper district that is changing the Milan skyline. The **Unicredit Headquarters/31**, **Vertical Forest/30** and **Diamond Tower/35** buildings, connected through a carefully designed course of mainly pedestrian open spaces, cover a range of functions including residential and office buildings, shopping centres and cultural centres. The circuit also includes **Palazzo Lombardia/28**, the new Regional Authority administrative seat, and the Piazza Duca d'Aosta, overlooked by the **Central Station/26** and the Pirelli **Skyscraper/25**.

Tour III - Consolidated urban areas

The third tour refers to the historical outskirts of the city and the consolidated urban areas. This was composed of a series of villages, mainly of medium density, located outside the Circonvallazione esterna ring road and sometimes quite a distance from one another. To the south, this circuit includes the **Università Bocconi/48**, composed of a complex built over a seventy-year period, and to the northwest, the Corso Sempione axis, where the **Casa Rustici/38** and the **Edificio per abitazioni INA/39**, are located. Close by are the new towers that make up the **Citylife/40** complex.

Tour IV - Greater Milan - North East

This tour covers the zone between the Circonvallazione esterna and the tangenziali ring road systems and also includes the boroughs of the Milanese hinterland. Some of the city's most important industrial, publishing and commercial companies are located in the northeast, including the **RCS/57**, **Mondadori/55**, **3M/54** and **Campari/59** headquarters. This is also the Bicocca area, site of one of Europe's greatest urban redevelopment projects, and home to the **Teatro degli Arcimboldi/60**, and the headquarters of **Pirelli RE/60** and **Deutsche Bank/61**.

Tour V - Greater Milan

The other zones of Greater Milan zone are home to several service industrial areas. Among these, to the south is the new **Milanofiori/80/81** district, composed of a series of new residential and office buildings, and to the southeast is the Comune of San Donato Milanese, hub of the **ENI/83** headquarters. The districts in the tours IV and V have been the scene of several very important experiments in innovative housing projects, including the buildings constructed as a result of the **Living in Milan competitions/56/65/73**, and the new residential complex in **Via Cenni/76**.

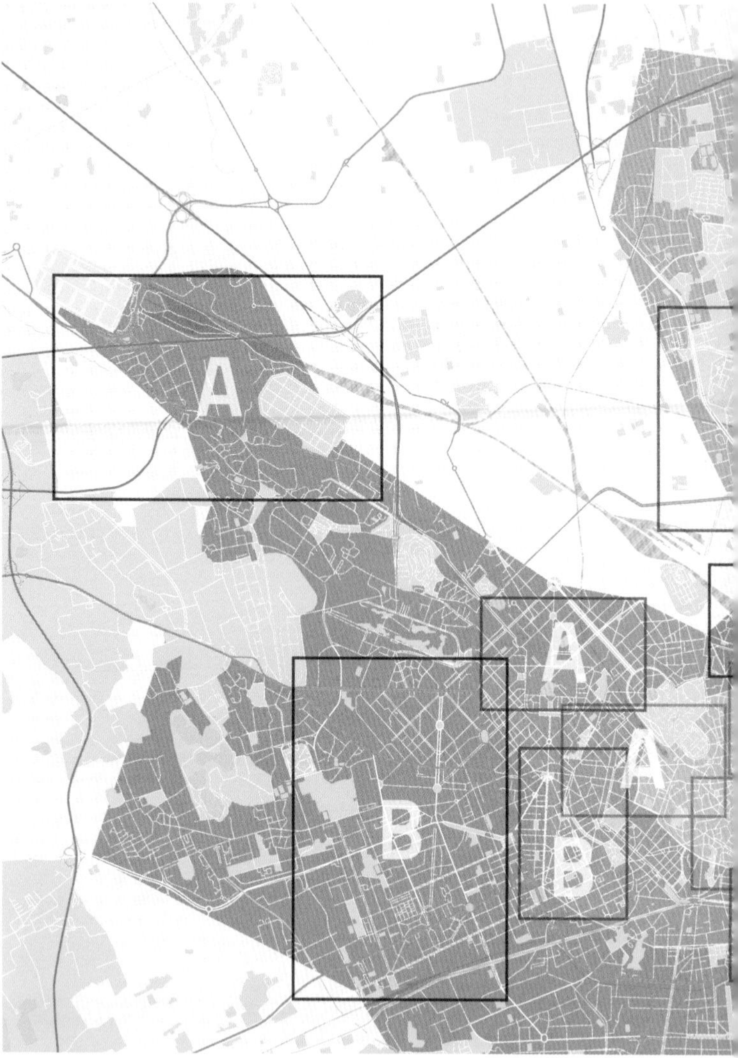
A
A
A
B
B

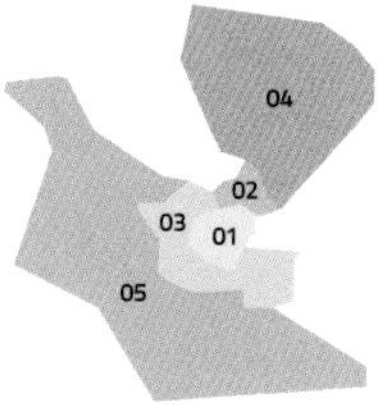

Routes

01. Milan City Centre
02. Garibaldi-
Repubblica-
Porta Venezia
03. Consolidated urban areas
04. Greater Milan –
North East
05. Greater Milan

Milan City Centre

01. Palazzo dell'Arte
02. Castello Sforzesco
03. Renovation of the Milan Metropolitan stations for lines 1 and 2
04. Santa Maria delle Grazie
05. Sant'Ambrogio

D
Basilica di San Simpliciano
Torre Branca
Viale Gadio
Corso Garibaldi
01
Triennale di Milano
Parco Sempione
Piccolo Teatro Studio Melato
Piccolo Teatro Strehler
Lanza
ilio Zola
Viale Moliere
Via Mercato
Castello Sforzesco
Foro Bonaparte
02
Studio Museo Achille Castiglioni
Via Giacomo Leopardi
Via Pietro Paleocapa
o Saffi
Piazza Castello
Via Cusani
Milano Cadorna
Fs
Cairoli
Largo Cairoli
03
Cadorna F.n.
4
occaccio
Foro Buonaparte
Via S. Giovanni sul Muro
Hotel Palazzo Segreti
Via Caradosso
Via Vincenzo Monti
Via Carducci
Corso Magenta
Via Meravigli
La Brisa
Via S. Maria Fulcorina
Piazza Affari
Via Sant'Agnese
Via Brisa
Via Santa Valeria
Piazza Sant'Ambrogio
Via Carducci
Via Cappuccio
Via Sant'Orsola
Via S. Maurilio
Museo Nazionale della Scienza e della Tecnologia
05
Quattroassociati
Basilica di Sant'Ambrogio
0 m
100 m
250 m

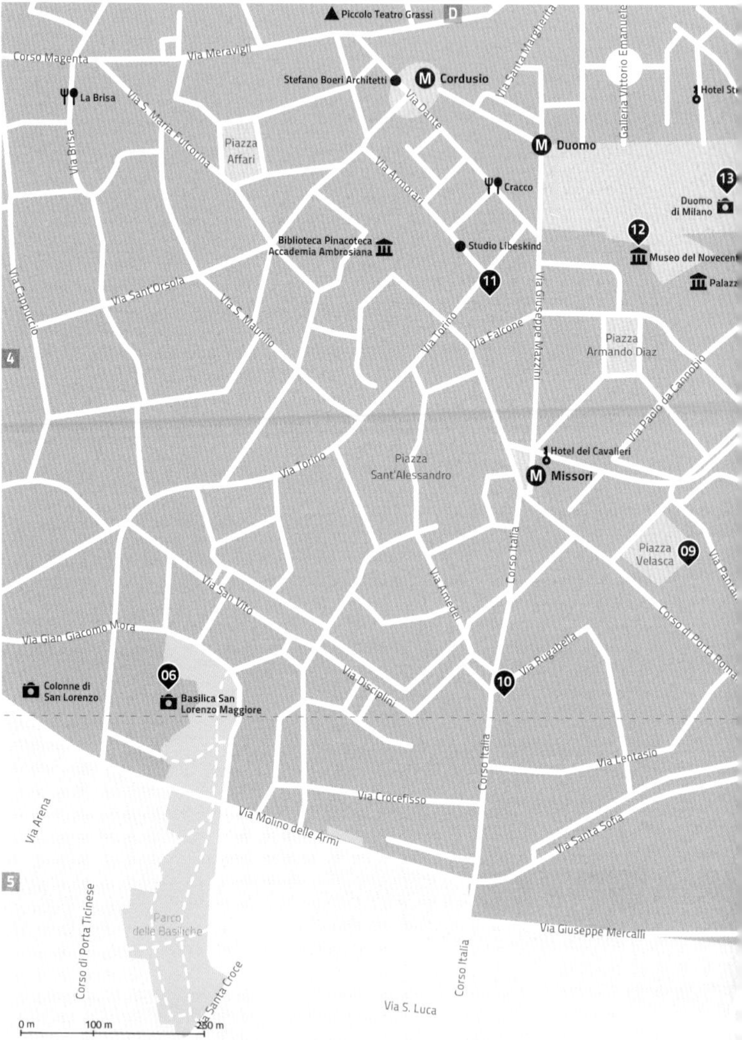

Piccolo Teatro Grassi
D
Corso Magenta
Via Meravigli
Stefano Boeri Architetti
Cordusio
Via Santa Margherita
Galleria Vittorio Emanuele
Hotel St
La Brisa
Via S. Maria Fulcorina
Via Dante
Piazza Affari
Duomo
Via Brisa
Via Armorari
Cracco
13
Duomo di Milano
Biblioteca Pinacoteca Accademia Ambrosiana
Studio Libeskind
12
Museo del Novecen
Palazz
11
Via Cappuccio
Via Sant'Orsola
Via S. Maurilio
Via Torino
Via Falcone
Via Giuseppe Mazzini
Piazza Armando Diaz
4
Via Paolo da Cannobio
Hotel dei Cavalieri
Via Torino
Piazza Sant'Alessandro
Missori
Piazza Velasca
09
Corso Italia
Via Pantan
Via San Vito
Via Amedei
Corso di Porta Roma
Via Gian Giacomo Mora
Via Rugabella
06
10
Colonne di San Lorenzo
Basilica San Lorenzo Maggiore
Via Disciplini
Via Lentasio
Corso Italia
Via Crocefisso
Via Molino delle Armi
Via Arena
Via Santa Sofia
5
Corso di Porta Ticinese
Parco delle Basiliche
Via Giuseppe Mercalli
Corso Italia
Via Santa Croce
Via S. Luca
0 m
100 m
250 m

Milan City Centre

06. San Lorenzo Maggiore
07. Casa della Meridiana
08. Ospedale Maggiore - Ca' Granda
09. The Velasca Tower
10. Residential and office block complex in Corso Italia
11. Santa Maria presso San Satiro
12. Museo del Novecento
13. Duomo (Milan Cathedral)
16. Excelsior Milano

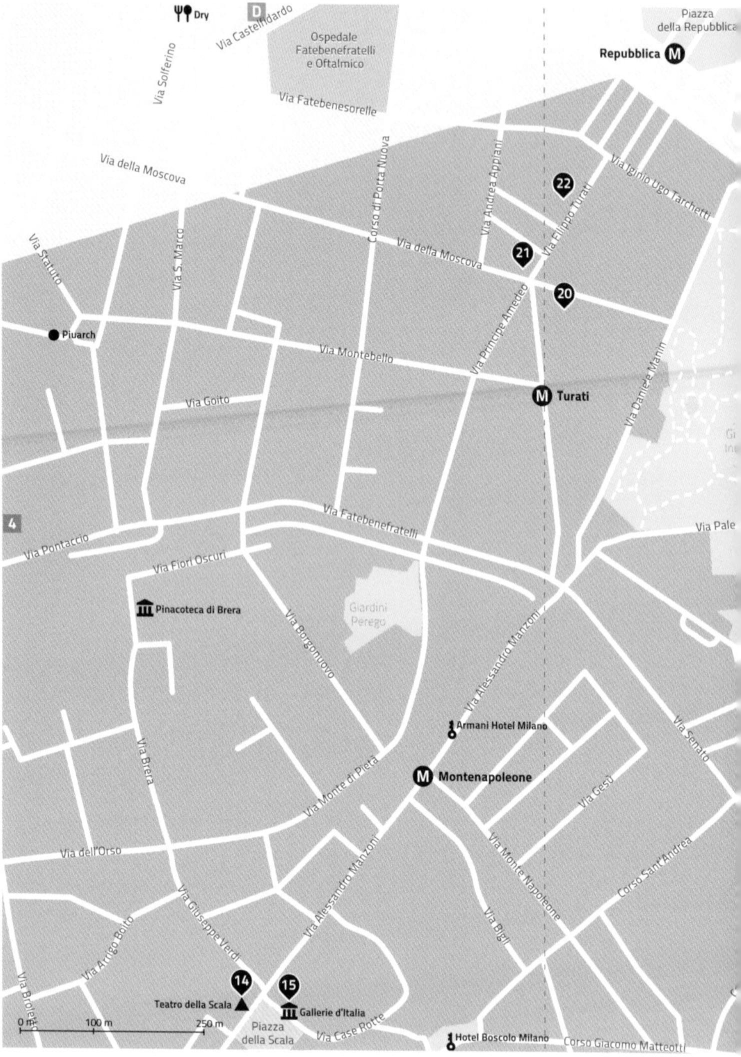
Dry
D
Via Castelfidardo
Ospedale Fatebenefratelli e Oftalmico
Via Solferino
Via Fatebenesorelle
Piazza della Repubblica
Repubblica
Via della Moscova
Corso di Porta Nuova
Via Andrea Appiani
22
Via Iginio Ugo Tarchetti
Via Filippo Turati
21
Via della Moscova
20
Via Statuto
Via S. Marco
Via Principe Amedeo
Piuarch
Via Montebello
Turati
Via Daniele Manin
Via Goito
4
Via Fatebenefratelli
Via Pale
Via Pontaccio
Via Fiori Oscuri
Pinacoteca di Brera
Giardini Perego
Via Borgonuovo
Via Alessandro Manzoni
Armani Hotel Milano
Via Senato
Via Brera
Montenapoleone
Via Monte di Pietà
Via Gesù
Via dell'Orso
Via Monte Napoleone
Corso Sant'Andrea
Via Giuseppe Verdi
Via Alessandro Manzoni
Via Bigli
Via Arrigo Boito
Via Broletto
14
15
Teatro della Scala
Gallerie d'Italia
0 m
100 m
250 m
Piazza della Scala
Via Case Rotte
Hotel Boscolo Milano
Corso Giacomo Matteotti

Milan City Centre

14. Renovation of the Teatro alla Scala
15. Gallerie d'Italia - Piazza Scala
17. Villa Necchi Campiglio
18. Milan Planetarium
19. Padiglione di Arte Contemporanea
20. The Montecatini Office Building
21. Ca' Brütta
22. La Serenissima Office Building

01. Palazzo dell'Arte

Viale Emilio Alemagna 6
20121 Milan

open to public

www.triennale.it

M1
Cadorna

61
Viale Alemagna

The Palazzo dell'Arte, location of the Triennale since 1933 (transferred here from the original location, Villa Reale in Monza), is located inside Parco Sempione, on the boundary of the Ferrovie Nord property. In chronological order, it represents the last of the series of public monumental buildings composed of the Castello Sforzesco, the Arco della Pace and the Arena.
The building has a rectangular structure, and on one of the shorter sides is semi-circular theatre and gallery. There are two symmetrical porticos on the longer sides, accessing Viale Alemagna on one side and overlooking the Park on the other. The building has three storeys with very high ceilings, dimensioned to accommodate the staging for art exhibitions, and is composed of a reinforced concrete structure clad in traditional materials (Baveno pink granite) as well as more innovative elements (clinker).
The construction has undergone several interventions; the most recent being the Galleria della Triennale (by Gae Aulenti) to house spaces equipped for temporary exhibitions, and the common areas (by Michele De Lucchi) with the new bookshop, café-restaurant, and Museo del Design.

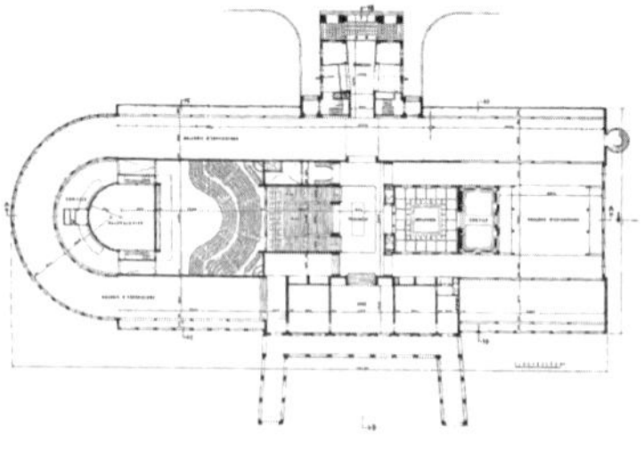

architects
Giovanni Muzio

type
museum

construction
1932-1933

02. Castello Sforzesco

Piazza Castello
27029 Milan

open to public

www.milanocastello.it

4
Piazza Castello

M1
Calroli

The Castello Sforzesco represents one of the most iconic symbols of Milan and is the multi-layered palimpsest of the city's historical events between the middle Ages and the present day.
In the mid-14th century, the first settlement consisted of a fortification built by the Visconti family and was destroyed with the extinction of the dynasty. It was rebuilt by Francesco I Sforza, who had it transformed into his residence; this was followed by a series of changes and extensions, including the Filarete Tower built in 1452, and the frescoes in the ducal apartments and the Sala delle Asse by Leonardo da Vinci, commissioned by Ludovico il Moro. After considerable damage caused by continuous battles, including the explosion inside the Filarete Tower (1521), the castle reassumed its military function under Spanish domination, with the construction of a new defence system (later demolished by Napoleon). It was restored in 1894 with the project by Luca Beltrami, who excavated the moat, removed the Ghirlanda defence walls, and rebuilt the tower.
After damage suffered during the Second World War, further interventions were carried out including the restoration of the internal Ducal Courtyard (1954-1956) and the Rocchetta courtyard (1963) by the BBPR studio and the restoration and staging of rooms for temporary exhibitions by Franco Albini, Franca Helg and Antonio Piva in 1974.

type
castle

construction
1360-1499,
1891-1905 (restoration)

03. Renovation of the Milan Metropolitan stations for lines 1 and 2

Stazioni della Metropolitana
20100 Milan

open to public

M1/M2
Metropolitan stations

The project involves the creation of a unifying and functional space (including permanent fixtures, services for the public and the station, stores and lighting) for the new Milan Metropolitan underground railway system, composed of pre-existing structures and with limited possibilities for any important structural or layout changes.
The vertical walls have been clad with a system of prefabricated modular panels in Silipol (a concrete, marble and stone conglomerate), fixed to a steel grid attached to the walls to enclose and cover all the electrical cables and firefighting systems. Attached on the panels, running along the whole length of the stations and mezzanine levels, is a horizontal metal plate strip with an enamel finish, printed with signs studied by the graphics expert Bob Noorda for maximum visibility by passengers inside the trains. The horizontal surfaces and mezzanine columns are finished in a dark colour to camouflage the irregularities of the concrete while all flooring is covered in large Pirelli studded rubber squares; the stairs in Serizzo ghiandone granite have curved 47.50 mm. tubular steel handrails.

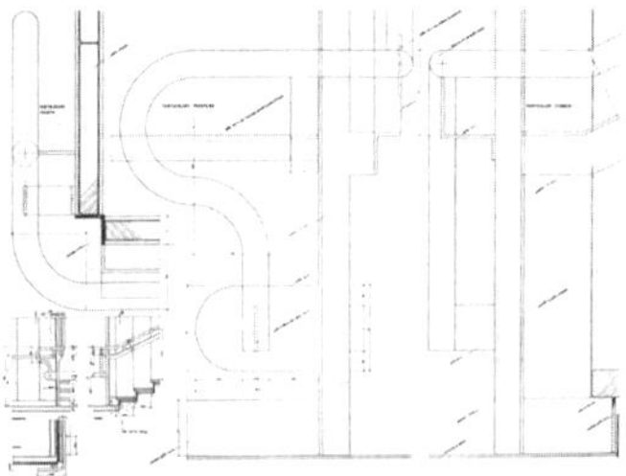

architects
Franco Albini
and Franca Helg

type
Metropolitan
stations

construction
1962-1964
and 1964-1969

04. Santa Maria delle Grazie

Piazza di Santa Maria delle Grazie
20123 Milan

open to public

www.grazieop.it

16
Santa Maria delle Grazie

The construction of the monastic complex of Santa Maria delle Grazie was carried out in several different stages. The church was built in 1463 by Guiniforte Solari for the Dominican order and designed according to traditional style with a central nave double the size of the side naves, with side chapels, gabled facade, and two-colour brick and plaster exterior. In 1492 Ludovico il Moro commissioned Bramante to rebuild the domed apse, intended as a commemorative chapel to the Sforza family featuring a cubic central volume with two semi-circular side exedras, a dome raised on a polygonal drum, and continuing the two colour exterior for coherence with the existing building. Also attributed to Bramante are the small square-shaped cloister with five brick arches on each side, and the old rectangular sacristy with vaulted ceilings. Adjacent to the church in the former refectory is the fresco of the Last Supper (1494-1498), the famous masterpiece of the Italian Renaissance by Leonardo da Vinci.

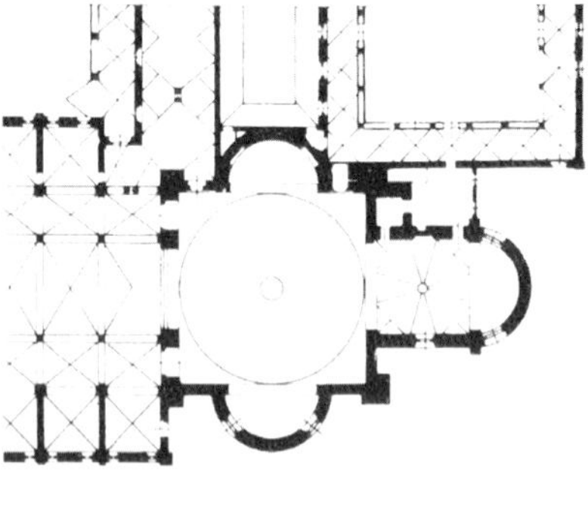

architects
Guiniforte Solari,
Donato Bramante

type
church

construction
1463-1469
and 1492-1497

05. Sant'Ambrogio

Piazza Sant'Ambrogio 15
20123 Milan

open to public

www.basilicasantambrogio.it

M2
Sant'Ambrogio

94
Sant'Ambrogio M2

The present basilica of Sant'Ambrogio, the major expression of Romanesque architecture in Milan, is the result of centuries of overlaid reconstruction interventions: the first church (Basilica Martyrum) was built between 379 and 386 by the bishop of Milan, St. Ambrose, in an area dedicated to the burial of numerous martyrs of the Roman persecutions. The complex assumed its current aspect between 1089 and 1099 when it underwent some radical transformations under the initiative of the bishop Anselm.
As well as the typical style of the classical basilica with its three naves, three apses, and four-sided portico, the building is unusual for its gabled facade, the use of locally sourced modest building materials (different coloured bricks, stone and plaster) and for the groin vaulted ceilings with ogives, one of the first examples of its kind in Europe.
The church is flanked by two square bell towers, the right hand tower called "the monks' tower" (IX century, and the oldest tower in Milan) and the left hand "Canons'" tower (XII century, and the taller of the two), with the same materials and design features as the four-sided portico.

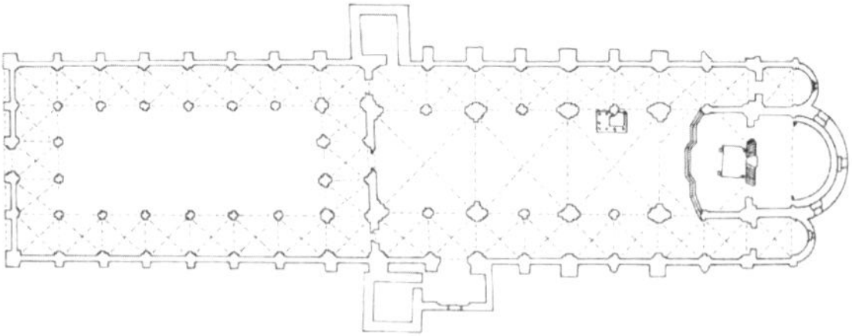

type
church

construction
1088-1099

06. San Lorenzo Maggiore

Corso di Porta Ticinese 39
20123 Milan

open to public

www.sanlorenzomaggiore.com

San Lorenzo is an early Christian basilica renowned for several centuries after its construction as the major central plan church of the Western Roman Empire.
The church has a square plan with protruding apses on each side forming a four-lobed cross, repeated interiorly by two-storeyed columns that separate the central space from the ambulatory around the perimeter, above which was later built the women's gallery.
While the 5th century chapel of Sant'Aquilino has maintained its original structure, the rest of the complex has been subject to several interventions and transformations over time. The most important change was made to the dome that collapsed in 1573 and was rebuilt in octagonal form by Martino Bassi, commissioned by the archbishop Carlo Borromeo. In later centuries, an entrance pronaos was added (1894) followed by the large square facing the city (1934), obtained with the demolition of the houses built around the previous courtyard.

94
Via De Amicis - Colonne di San Lorenzo

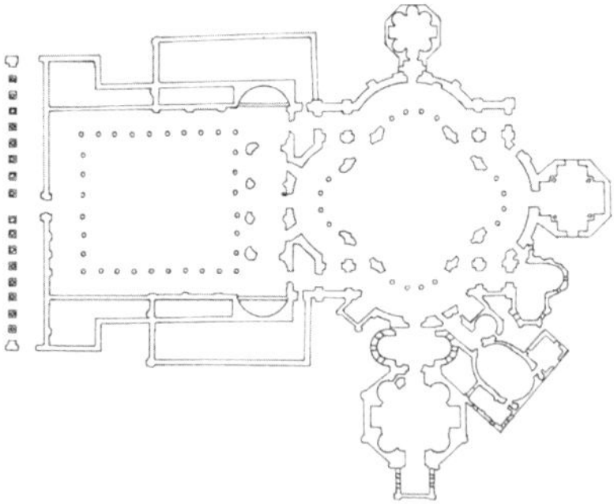

type
church

construction
4th century

07. Casa della Meridiana

Via Paolo Marchiondi 3,
Piazza Cardinal Ferrari
20122 Milan

external viewing only

94
Corso di Porta Romana - Via Santa Sofia

This residential building was named because of the sundial painted by the artist, Gigiotti Zanini, on the facade overlooking Via Marchiondi; it was built in the Giardino d'Arcadia, annexed to the Palazzo Melzi formerly Pertusati (destroyed during bombings in World War II) for which the town planning law of 1912 permitted a constructed volume greater than that later built; permission was also given to open up a street that would have divided the garden in two and sacrificed several beautiful trees.
The unified but complex structure clearly shows the influence of Adolf Loos (De Finetti was one of his students), and is composed of a series of terraces descending down to the garden, each terrace bordered with string-course moulding. The apartments differ in size and layout, and even the furnishings were designed according to the proprietors' needs and tastes.
The intervention in the Giardino d'Arcadia was completed with a condominium constructed in Via San Calimero 17 (1930). The facade on the street shows the different uses of space, with offices in the base of the building, "villas" on the top two floors, and apartments in the middle floors.

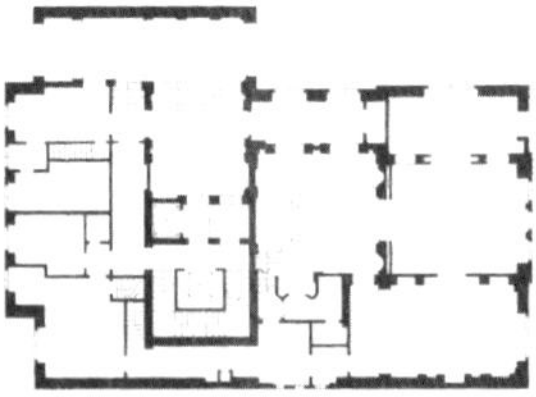

architects
Giuseppe De Finetti

type
residential

construction
1924-1925

08. Ospedale Maggiore - Ca' Granda

Via Francesco Sforza,
Via Laghetto,
Via Festa del Perdono
20122 Milan

open to public

www.unimi.it

77/94
Via Sforza -
Via Andreani

This historical complex which has had a very strong influence on the concept of large-scale public building design, is the first example of a modern hospital and the first example of a layout composed of a sequence of square courtyards set in cross formation. The Ospedale Maggiore was commissioned by Francesco Sforza to gather all the smaller hospitals spread around the city in a single unit. It was composed of two separate square constructions divided into a cross formation that separated the various wings according to disease to avoid contamination. The wings met in a rectangular space that was to have held a church in the centre of the cross formation, but was later moved to the rear side. Certain changes and modifications were made to Filarete's initial project with successive interventions by Guiniforte Solari and Giovanni Antonio Amadeo, who changed the single lancet windows to rounded mullioned arched windows on the main facade, and by Francesco Maria Richini, who created the square form of the central courtyard.
Following the serious damage suffered during the bombing in 1943, the building was completely restored by Liliana Grassi with a project aimed at recovering as many of the original materials as possible. Since 1958, the building has been the seat of the Università degli Studi di Milano.

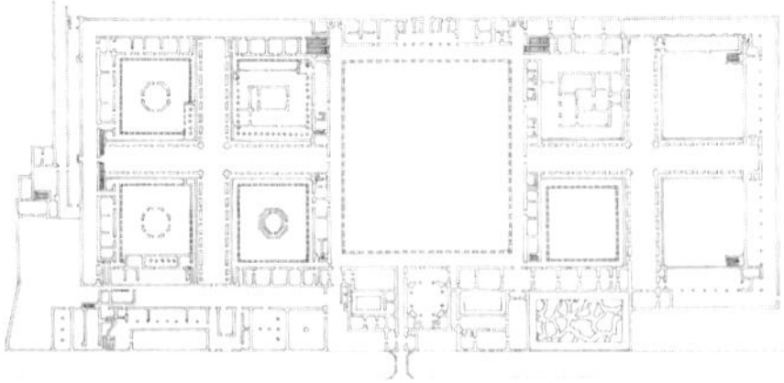

© Matteo Moscatelli

architects
Filarete, Guiniforte Solari,
Giovanni Antonio Amadeo,
Francesco Maria Richini,
Liliana Grassi (restoration)

type
university

construction
1456-1805,
1949-1985 (restoration)

09. The Velasca Tower

Piazza Velasca 5
20122 Milan

external viewing only

12/15/27
Via Albricci

M3
Missori

54
Via Albricci

The result of a long experimental route which led to formalising multiple alternatives in volume and construction, this building is emblematic of the research carried out by the BBPR studio on the relationship with pre-existent environmental and artistic elements, understood, not as a "naturalistic, imitative or analogical" agreement, but as "empathy with things that surround us", in which we should try to absorb the meaning within their composition.
From the forepart to the base, containing office and retail spaces and two underground floors for parking, the tower (106 metres tall) is composed of two parts. The lower part (19 floors) houses offices and office-habitation units, and the projecting upper seven floors are dedicated to apartments of various sizes and layouts (six are duplex apartments).
The reinforced concrete structure is protected with a cement and Veronese marble grit plaster finish. The section of the exposed columns is square on the ground floor, T-shaped on the third floor, and detached from the building facade for the last three levels of the lower part. The varied use of the internal spaces is underlined by a diversified layout for the openings on the facades, designed with certain variations for the residential floors, with a more regular grid pattern for the office floors.

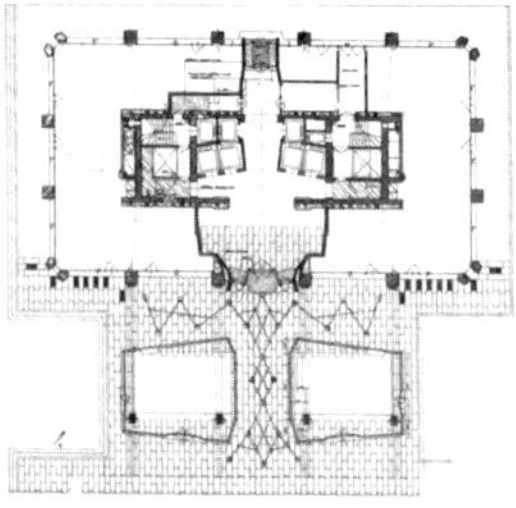

architects
BBPR, Arturo Danusso

type
residential, offices

construction
1951-1958

10. Residential and Office Block Complex in Corso Italia

Corso Italia 13-17,
Via Rugabella
20122 Milan

external viewing only

3/15
Corso Italia -
Missori M3

M3
Missori

This complex, built on a triangular plot, is composed of four buildings: a three-storeyed construction on Via Rugabella houses shops on the ground floor and offices on the upper two floors; set on top of this building is another eight-floor construction, originally designed for residential use, but today converted to office space; and on the opposite side of the private internal road is a further six-storey office block and internally in the plot, parallel to Corso Italia, is a twelve storey building.
Each building is distinguished by specific choices as far as dimension, orientation and style are concerned: the internal volume, with its lamellar configuration has a rounded corner facing south, and is divided in two by a slot, like the house-hotel in Via Corridoni (1946-1951). The building in Corso Italia, featuring a projecting tapered extremity, shows a different aspect on each side of the construction. There is a more introverted effect on the side facing the city centre to the north, and the side facing the suburbs to the south, is more extroverted in style.
The use of innovative materials, curtain wall and mobile internal partition walls for greater flexibility in arranging the internal layout demonstrates the considerable levels of constructive experimentation in this project design.

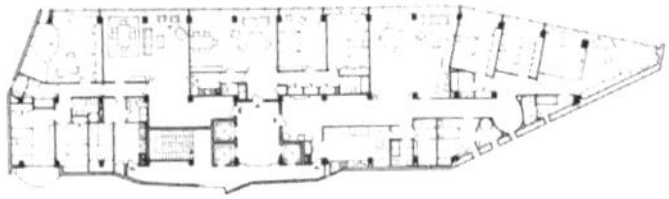

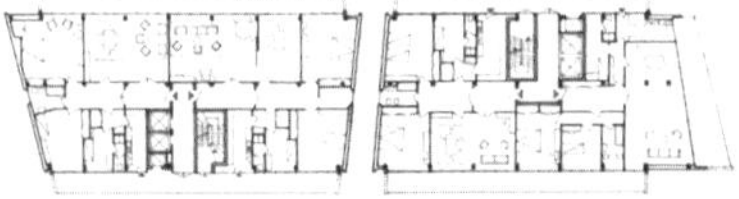

architects
Luigi Moretti

type
residential, offices

construction
1949-1955

11. Santa Maria presso San Satiro

Via Torino 17-19
20123 Milan

open to public

2/3/12/14/
16/19/24/27
Duomo M1 M3

M1/M3
Duomo

Santa Maria presso San Satiro is the first architectural work by Bramante in Milan and the result of an intervention that was to have included the construction of the church and the incorporation and restoration of the existing sacellum of San Satiro, commissioned by the archbishop Ansperto in the early middle Ages. It was composed of a "Greek cross" ground plan enclosed in a square set inside a circle.

The new construction was based on a triple nave with a Tau Cross form where the width was taken to the arms of the transept; the centre nave is covered with a coffered vaulted ceiling that recalls the influence of the church of Sant'Andrea in Mantua (1472-1494) by Leon Battista Alberti, while the right hand nave leads to the octagonal sacristy, an example of Renaissance architecture later transformed to become a Baptistery.

Very striking, and a precursor in the field of trompe l'oeil, is the optical illusion of a recessed archway painted in a space only 97 centimetres deep to obviate the lack of an apse caused by the passage of a street at the rear of the church.

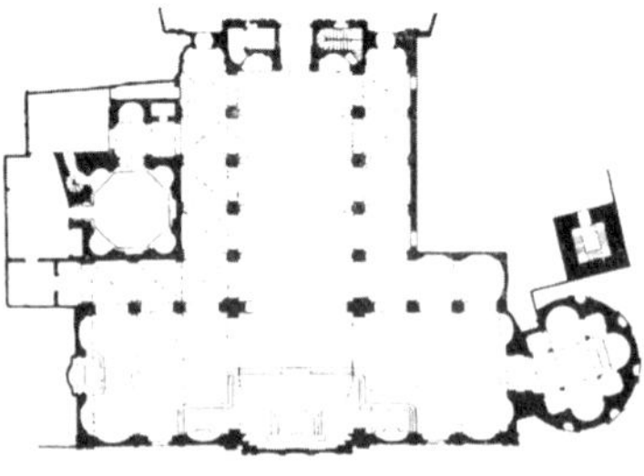

architects
Donato Bramante

type
church

construction
1476-1482

12. Museo del Novecento

Via Guglielmo Marconi 1
20122 Milan

open to public

www.museodelnovecento.org

2/3/12/14/
16/19/24/27
Duomo M1 M3

M1/M3
Duomo

The Museo del Novecento was created in order to address an obvious void in the panorama of public buildings in Milan: the absence of a museum dedicated to contemporary art.
In the final years of the last century, it was proposed to set up an exhibition space in the "dark zone" of Piazza Duomo in the Arengario Palace, built in the 1930s by Griffini, Magistretti, Muzio and Portaluppi. In 1999, a competition was announced for the transformation of the building. The project was awarded to Studio Rota, whose reconstruction work carved out a surface of 8 thousand square metres, 6 thousand of which was dedicated to exhibition space.
Among the aims of the project, the objective was to give the new complex a recognisable and attractive image: one of the elements with major impact is the connecting spiral ramp that leads from the subway entrance up through the building to the Sala delle Colonne, a monumental space that marks the beginning of the itinerary through the museum exhibition spaces. Built in self-supporting glass, the space reaches its peak in the section dedicated to Lucio Fontana that houses his neon lasso composition, a further element in the continuous dialogue between the Museum and the Piazza del Duomo.

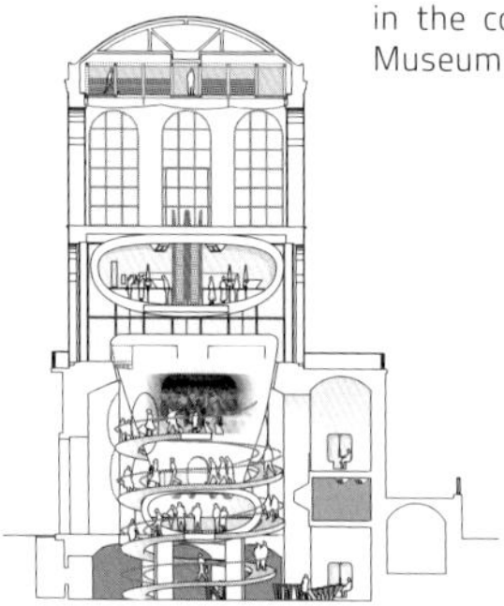

© Italo Rota

architects
Studio Italo Rota & Partners

type
museum

construction
2002-2010

13. Duomo (Milan Cathedral)

Piazza del Duomo
20122 Milan

open to public

www.duomomilano.it

2/3/12/14/
16/19/24/27
Duomo M1 M3

M1/M3
Duomo

The fourth largest church in Europe, the Duomo rises in a space that in ancient times was the location of two churches, the Basilica di Santa Maria Maggiore (initially englobed in the new construction) and the Basilica di Santa Tecla.
The very long construction period, in the early stages inspired by the central European late Gothic style, is evident in the succession of styles on the richly ornate front facade that includes the 16th century interventions by Pellegrino Tibaldi, 17th century works by Francesco Maria Richini, and the additions in the 19th century commissioned by Napoleon. The majesty of the building, with the Madonnina (the gold Virgin statue placed in 1774) and overall height of 108.50 metres, is accentuated even further by the internal and external facing in pink Candoglia marble extracted from the quarry in Val d'Ossola and transported to Milan by crossing Lake Maggiore, the Ticino River, and the Navigli canals as far as the present day Via Laghetto; the cathedral is famous for its spires, the oldest of which (Guglia Carelli) dates back to 1404.
The piazza in front of the cathedral is overlooked on the north side by the Galleria Vittorio Emanuele II (1865-1877), the cross-shaped covered gallery built by Giuseppe Mengoni and emblematic of the construction methods using iron and glass that were fashionable in Europe at the time; on the southern side is Palazzo Reale, former city administration building, and today a space for temporary art exhibitions and events.

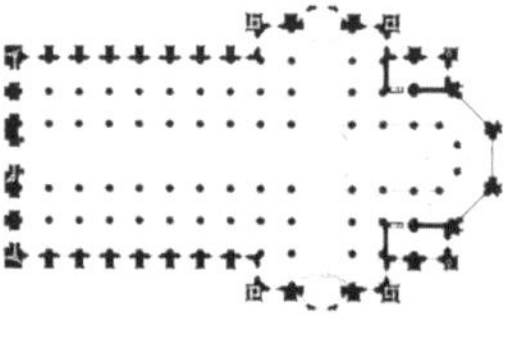

© Matteo Moscatelli

type
church

construction
1386-1892

14. Renovation of the Teatro alla Scala

Via Filodrammatici 2
20121 Milan

open to public

www.teatroallascala.org

1
Via Manzoni - Teatro alla Scala

M1/M3
Duomo

The Teatro alla Scala (1776-1778) designed by Giuseppe Piermarini, is one of the most important opera houses in the world, renowned for the famous artists and prestigious works that have been performed here; it is the traditional model of the "Italian Style" theatre, with its horse-shoe auditorium, balconies and opera boxes to replace the tiered bench seating, and the greater depth in the stage space.
The renovation project was proposed following a palimpsest of transformations and additions that had continued almost since the theatre had been built. The new constructions include an ellipsoid services structure, built on the roof of the Casino Ricordi, to house dressing rooms, changing rooms, offices, and the new theatre cafeteria, and the parallelepiped structure of the new fly tower (38 metres high) set back from the façade in Via Verdi. The fly tower houses the new theatrical rigging machinery, and over the back stage, the ballet and chorus rehearsal rooms. The conservation work performed on the forestage of the theatre, the foyer, the entrance, the main theatre auditorium, and the Casino Ricordi, was composed of a range of specialised restoration interventions plus careful cleaning of the damaged elements.

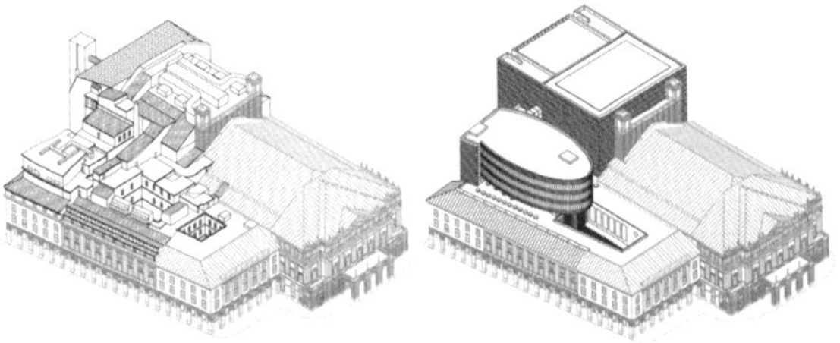

architects
Mario Botta,
Elisabetta Fabbri

type
theatre

construction
2002-2004

15. Gallerie d'Italia - Piazza Scala

Piazza della Scala 6
20121 Milan

open to public

www.gallerieditalia.com

1
Via Manzoni -
Teatro alla Scala

M1/M3
Duomo

This intervention involved the connecting of four historical buildings, Anguissola (1775-1778), Antona Traversi (1829), Brentani (1829) and Beltrami (1906-1911), and their transformation into an exhibition space to show the collection of 19th century art belonging to Intesa San Paolo and Fondazione Cariplo, as well as the bank's 20th century Italian artworks; the space will also host important temporary exhibitions. The access entrance is located in Piazza della Scala, where the interior of the Banca Commerciale Italiana was adapted without altering the original style and character. The itinerary continues through a sequence of exhibition rooms separated by a glassed courtyard, and leads to a café and bookshop on the corner between Piazza della Scala and Via Manzoni. Wooden surfaces, oak for the flooring and cedar for the service area furnishing, create a unified effect, while the passage from one building to another is marked by interventions that are more subtle and less visible.

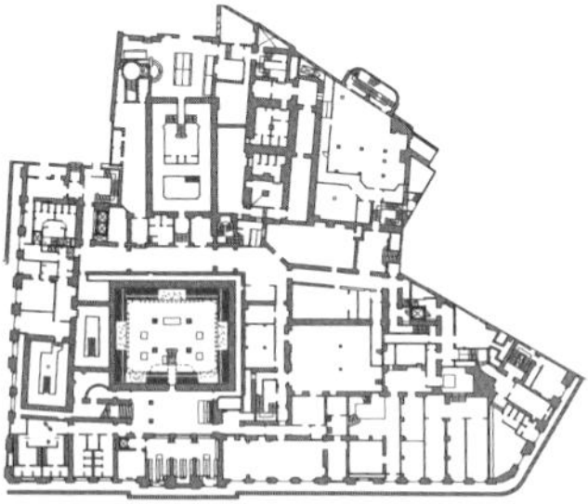

architects
Michele De Lucchi

type
museum

construction
2010-2012

16. Excelsior Milano

Galleria del Corso 4
20122 Milan

open to public

www.excelsiormilano.com

15/23
Piazza Fontana

M1/M3
Duomo

This intervention involved the transformation of the two former movie theatres, Excelsior and Mignon, into a concept store selling high-end fashion, food, and design. The store covers a surface of 4,000 square metres on seven levels and one of the main features is its experimental visual perception effects.

Reflections from special paints used on the internal walls of the existing movie theatre and the LED screens placed along the external edge of the new attic spaces detached from the main building create environments that change in appearance and perspective in continuation. Particular attention has been paid to the arched openings on the facades facing Via Passarella, linked with the entrance to the Galleria del Corso; horizontal aluminium slats, with a dull satin finish in the upper part, and shiny mirror finish at the bottom have been positioned in front of the openings. These slats reflect the images that appear on the screens and because of the multiple angle settings, allow a glimpse of the internal spaces of the store from different angles and distances.

© Ateliers Jean Nouvel

architects
Ateliers Jean Nouvel

type
commercial

construction
2010-2011

17. Villa Necchi Campiglio

Via Wolfango Amedeo Mozart 14
20122 Milan

open to public

www.fondoambiente.it

M1
Palestro

94
Corso Venezia - Via Senato

Villa Necchi Campiglio was designed and built by Piero Portaluppi between 1932 and 1935 for Nedda and Gigina Necchi and the husband of the latter, Angelo Campiglio. As well as the villa, the complex includes a large garden, swimming pool and guardian's lodge.
The internal layout of the house follows the traditional style of the affluent villas of the time, with a different purpose for each floor: the basement floor was for the service areas, the ground floor for reception, the first floor, bedrooms and bathrooms, and the attic level for the servants' quarters. Portaluppi's architectural design was based on refined streamlined spaces, and was indicative of the architect's renewed style, demonstrated in the 1930s. The rooms are designed with carefully harmonised combinations of materials and colours, and a composite of the regular geometrical elements such as semi-circles in the entrance and the rhombus patterns on the ceilings.
The changes made later by Tomaso Buzzi after the war gave the villa a more classical aspect. Since 2001, the villa has become the property of FAI – Fondo Ambiente Italiano that has been responsible for the restoration work and transformation into a house-museum open to the public since 2008.

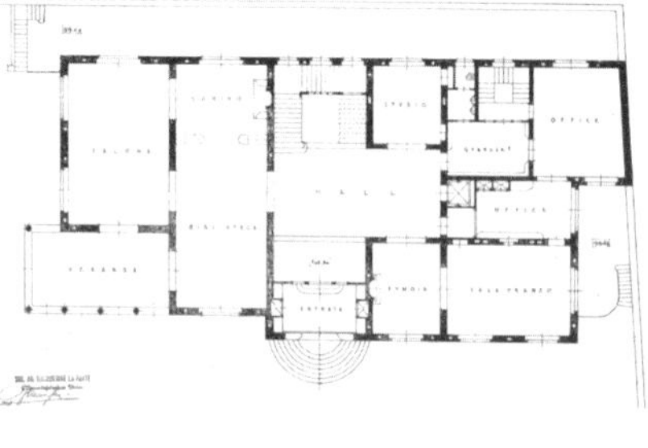

© Fondazione Piero Portaluppi, Milano

architects
Piero Portaluppi

type
museum

construction
1932-1935

18. Milan Planetarium

Corso Venezia 57
20121 Milan

open to public

www.comune.milano.it/planetario

9
Porta Venezia M1

M1
Porta Venezia

Donated to the city by the publisher, Ulrico Hoepli, the Planetarium is located in an area within the Corso Venezia public park conceded by the Milan Municipal Authorities. It was the result of collaboration between Emilio Bianchi, director of the Brera Observatory and scientific head of the operation, and Piero Portaluppi, responsible for the architectural design.
The octagonal building is crowned by a semi-spherical dome, 20 metres in diameter, inside which the night sky and astronomical phenomena is realistically reproduced by a projection system placed in the centre of the building. Around the perimeter are several spaces for storage, offices, a small astronomical museum, and bathroom facilities. The spherical roof houses acoustic, structural and maintenance equipment, and the external surface is coated with a layer of tar and ground marble that gives the dome its characteristic green colour. The building is clad in stone (ceppo di Albino and Crevola d'Ossola) with plastered sections. It is accessed by a wide staircase that recalls the entry to a temple through a classical pronaos with four grooved plinthless columns and crowned by a triangular tympanum.

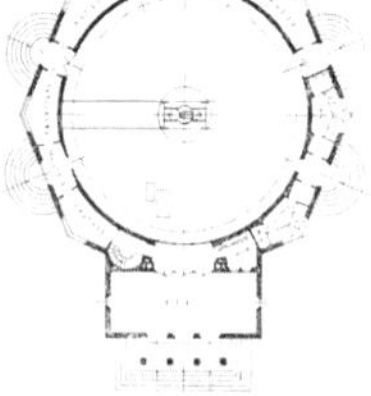

architects
Piero Portaluppi

type
planetarium

construction
1929-1930

19. Padiglione di Arte Contemporanea

Via Palestro 14
20121 Milan

open to public

www.pacmilano.it

1
Piazza Cavour

M1
Palestro

Symbol of the cultural re-birth of the city after the Second World War, the PAC was built in the location of the stables of the Villa Reale (which had been destroyed by the bombing in 1943) to house the collection of art of the XX century, belonging to the Milan Municipality.
The rooms are designed with different spatial layouts and in relation to the natural daylight. The paintings are on show on an upper level, lit by overhead skylights; the drawings and prints are hung in the balconied gallery on the first floor that can be accessed by a staircase with staggered steps, while the sculpture exhibition opens out to the exterior in full daylight with "I Sette Savi" by Fausto Melotti.
The building underwent extensive restructuration work in 1979 and in 1996, following a terrorist attack that almost destroyed the building. Gardella, the original architect, making a few modifications to the former design, rebuilt it. The ceiling was built with aluminium slats, and new technical equipment and a new lighting system were also added.

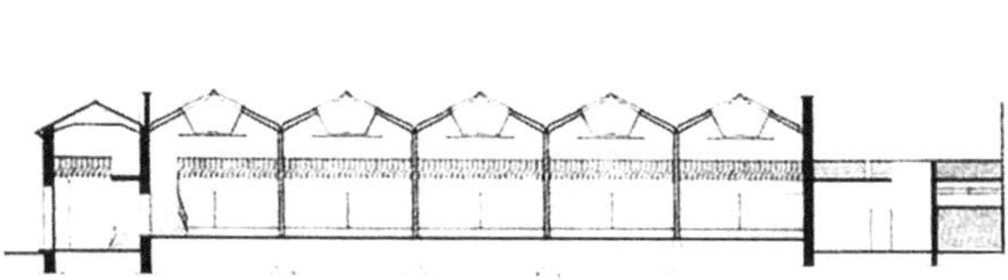

architects
Ignazio Gardella

type
museum

construction
1948-1954

20. The Montecatini Office Building

Largo Guido Donegani 2,
Via Principe Amedeo 2
20121 Milan

external viewing only

1
Largo Donegani - Turati M3

M3
Turati

43
Turati M3

The complex was built on two adjacent city blocks, but in two separate stages. The first construction, built between the two world wars, was composed of volumes of different heights arranged in an H-shape layout, with facades featuring aluminium window frames and green Appuan marble cladding; the complex design features continued in the interior where every component, including desks, seating, lighting and elevator cabins, was designed personally for this space.
After the bombings of the Second World War, the main building was rebuilt and raised a further floor despite the opposition by Ponti, who used this experience to conduct research into the completed form, as a base for his successive projects.
The second building repeated certain composition aspects and materials used on the first building apart from the use of Apuan marble for the street facades and the white mosaic tiling for the interiors. The complex is composed of two low buildings, and a tall element that connects the two and is set back from the street to create a filter towards the exhibition gallery. A third wing defines an internal courtyard.

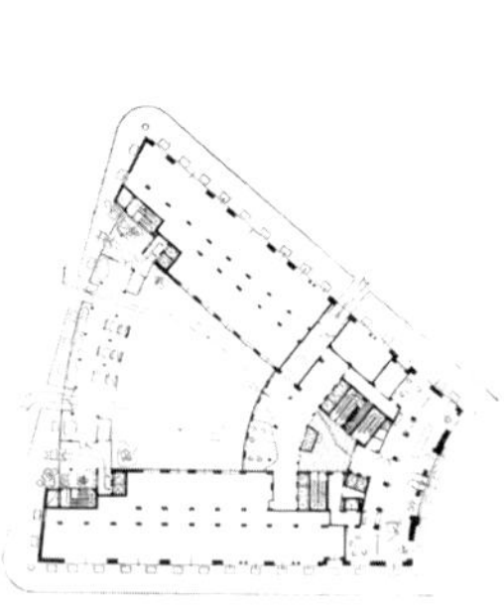

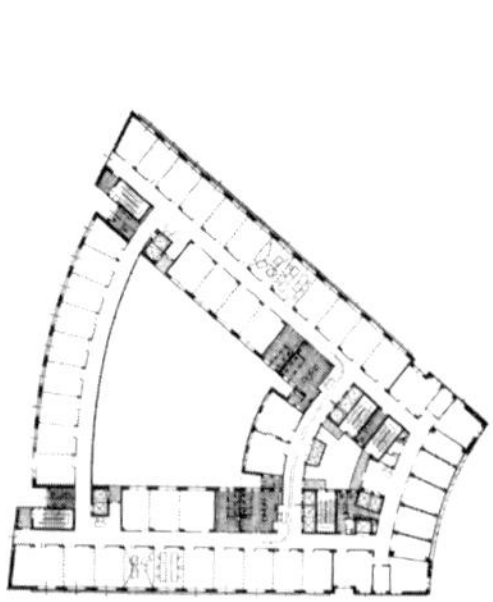

© Matteo Moscatelli

architects
Gio Ponti, Antonio Fornaroli
and Eugenio Soncini

type
offices

construction
1935-1938
and 1947-1951

21. Ca' Brütta

Via della Moscova 12,
Via Turati, Via Appiani,
Via Cavalieri
20121 Milan

external viewing only

1
Largo Donegani - Turati M3

M3
Turati

43
Turati M3

This residential complex represents the professional debut of Giovanni Muzio, and takes its name ("Ugly House") from the number of controversies that arose after its construction; it was considered a shameless use of classical sources, and as far as its composition was concerned, lacking in interest in "finding a balance and harmony in the distribution of the large number of openings".
The complex occupies an entire city block and is composed of two buildings, one longer linear block and a building built to enclose a courtyard; both blocks are separated by a private street, but connected by an arch that links the two extremities. The design has innovative technical and layout solutions such as the elimination of light wells, the division of the apartments into reception areas, owners' and domestics' quarters, and the care taken with the orientation of the main rooms.
The facades are divided into three horizontal bands in different materials; stone for the bottom floor, grey stucco for the middle floor and Venetian marble stucco finish for the top floors.

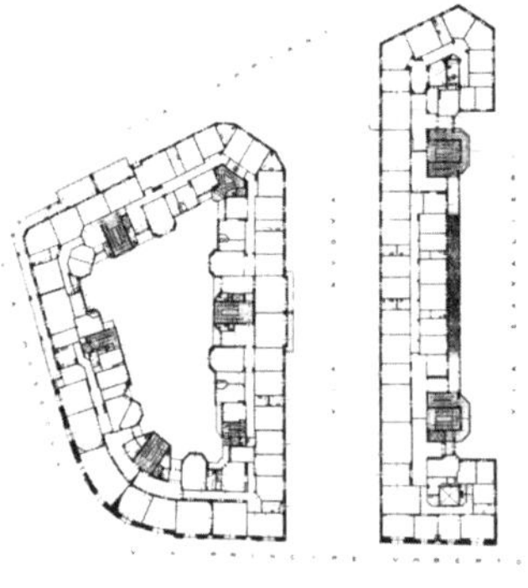

architects
Giovanni Muzio,
Vittorino Colonnese
and Pier Fausto Barelli

type
residential

construction
1919-1922

22. La Serenissima Office Building

Via Filippo Turati 25-27
20121 Milan

external viewing only

1
Largo Donegani - Turati M3

M3
Turati

43
Turati M3

This project refers to the renovation of an existing building, known as "Palazzo Campari", designed by the Soncini brothers, Ermenegildo and Eugenio, in the 1960s. It has a five storey curtain wall facade facing Via Turati, and three floors on Via Cavalieri overlooking Ca' Brütta.
The intervention involved bringing the construction up to current energy and construction standards: the perimeter facades were moved back from street level, creating cavities to eliminate heat bridges, and a series of perforated press-folded, burnished, aluminium boxes were added to the façade, acting as "nocturnal lanterns" giving the building strong visual impact when lit at night. The ground floor footprint was increased, while leaving the internal green-planted courtyard intact according to the original design. Inside the building, the project aimed at creating new distribution and increased flexibility in the internal office spaces by optimising the horizontal and vertical space.

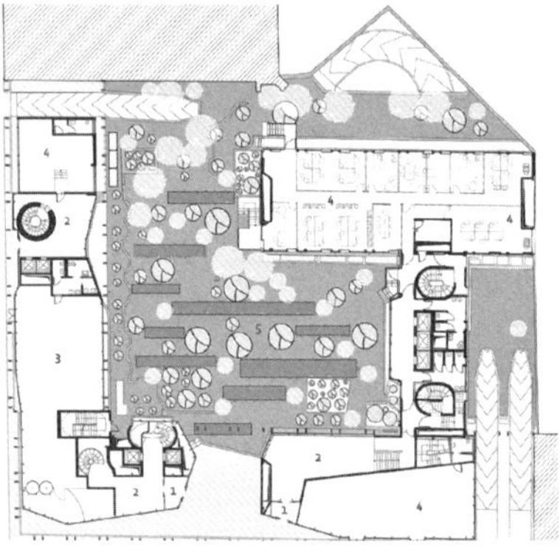

© Park Associati

architects
Park Associati

type
offices

construction
2010-2012

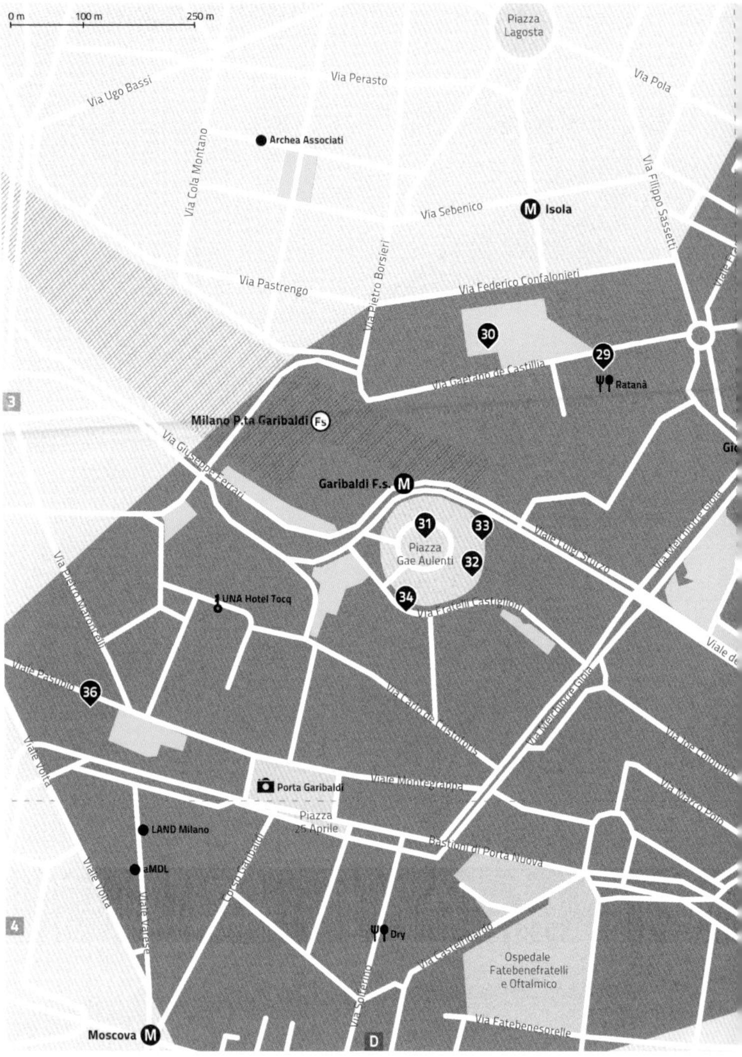
0 m
100 m
250 m
Piazza Lagosta
Via Perasto
Via Pola
Via Ugo Bassi
Archea Associati
Via Cola Montano
Via Filippo Sassetti
Via Sebenico
Isola
Via Pietro Borsieri
Via Pastrengo
Via Federico Confalonieri
30
29
Via Gaetano de Castillia
Ratanà
3
Milano P.ta Garibaldi
Via Giuseppe Ferrari
Garibaldi F.s.
31
33
Piazza Gae Aulenti
32
Viale Luigi Sturzo
Via Melchiorre Gioia
34
Via Fratelli Castiglioni
UNA Hotel Tocq
Via Pietro Maroncelli
Viale Pasubio
36
Via Carlo de Cristoforis
Via Melchiorre Gioia
Via Joe Colombo
Viale Volta
Porta Garibaldi
Viale Montegrappa
Via Marco Polo
Piazza 25 Aprile
Bastioni di Porta Nuova
LAND Milano
aMDL
Viale Volta
Corso Garibaldi
Viale Varese
4
Dry
Via Castelfidardo
Ospedale Fatebenefratelli e Oftalmico
Via Solferino
Via Fatebenesorelle
Moscova
D

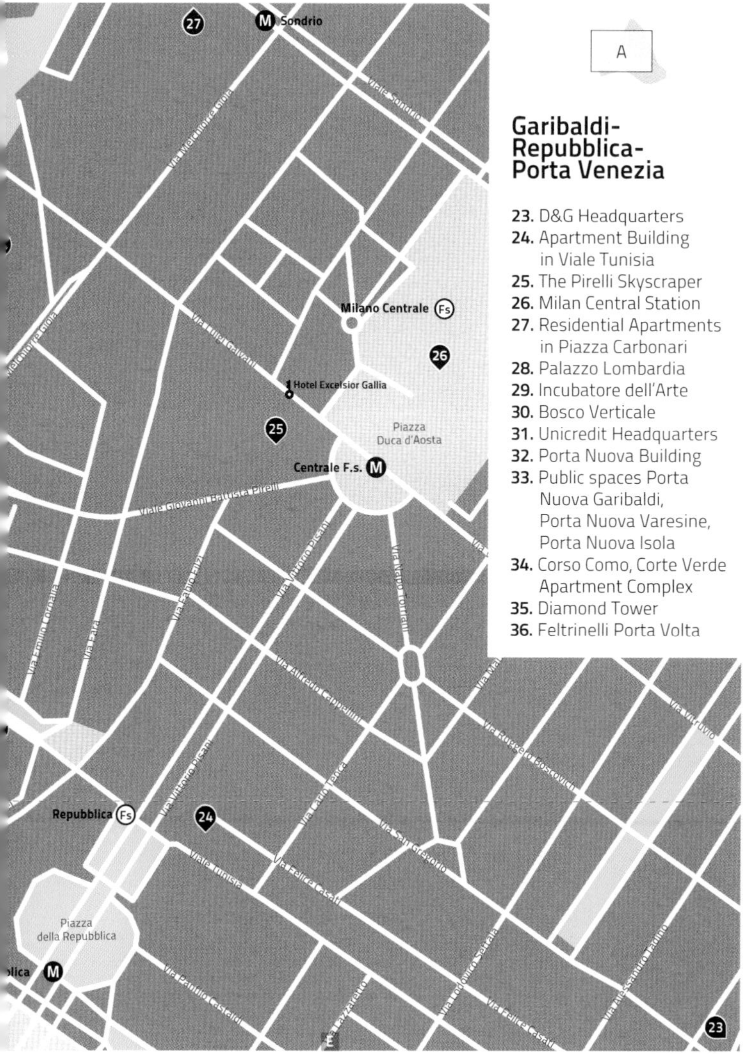

Garibaldi-Repubblica-Porta Venezia

23. D&G Headquarters
24. Apartment Building in Viale Tunisia
25. The Pirelli Skyscraper
26. Milan Central Station
27. Residential Apartments in Piazza Carbonari
28. Palazzo Lombardia
29. Incubatore dell'Arte
30. Bosco Verticale
31. Unicredit Headquarters
32. Porta Nuova Building
33. Public spaces Porta Nuova Garibaldi, Porta Nuova Varesine, Porta Nuova Isola
34. Corso Como, Corte Verde Apartment Complex
35. Diamond Tower
36. Feltrinelli Porta Volta

23. D&G Headquarters

Via Giuseppe Broggi 23
20129 Milan

external viewing only

M1
Lima

60
Via Eustachi -
Via Maiocchi

Just off the elegant Via Morgagni are the headquarters and showroom of the fashion designers, Dolce e Gabbana. The project designed by Piuarch is based on extremely sober lines to harmonise the link between new and pre-existent, between the white prism on the corner and the 19th century building alongside. Vertical sheets of translucent glass are positioned in a closely regular grid arrangement on the urban facade, creating a sense of depth on the transparent walls and rhythmically defining the stratified layers of the elements on show. The internal slab floors have a sense of lightness thanks to the choice of covering materials, including the top floor, but which like an outer skin, protects and interrupts the continuity with the volumes created on the roof (that house the restaurant and a series of small open terraces). The building support columns are set under the recessed facades to create a form of negative space base. The internal open courtyard with its white river stones and miniature rolling hills creates a bond between the existing and new buildings. The internal courtyard facade is faced with Namibia white marble. In this case, the abstract interpretation does not deny the different architectural aspects, but is used deliberately to redefine them.

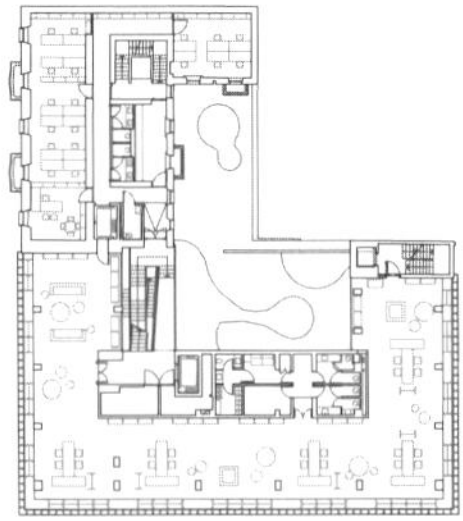

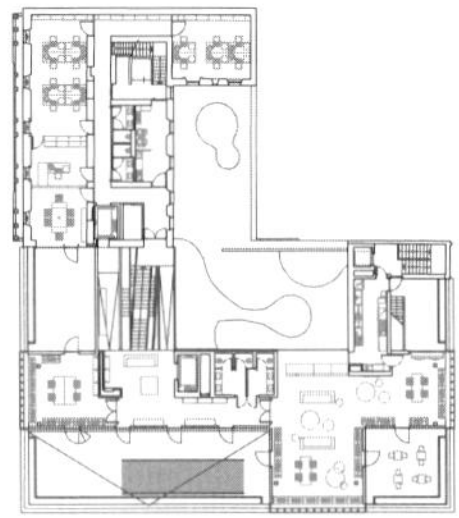

architect	type	construction
Piuarch	offices	2005-2006

24. Apartment Building in Viale Tunisia

Viale Tunisia 50
20124 Milan

external viewing only

M3
Repubblica

S1/S2/S5/S6/S13
Repubblica

Reading the list of projects designed by Asnago and Vender for Milan is like reconstructing the historical and cultural transition experienced by the city between the rationalist period and the years of the economic boom.
The apartment building in Viale Tunisia is representative of the "silent" work of the two architects, directed at formal research and consistently correct facades: a timeless style, result of a refined professional culture whose echo reverberates constantly throughout Milan. The grid composition dominates the entire structure of the facade divided into two distinct sections: the lower floors have a regular grid pattern of narrower windows and a large opening on the corner with the entrance, and today also includes store windows; the upper part features long balconies that protrude from under the windows with recessed walls that give a sense of lightness to the building as a whole.
The building is entirely clad in travertine stone, conveying a sculptural effect, almost as if it were an enlarged piece of moulding from some piece of classical architecture, filtered through the process of modern project design.

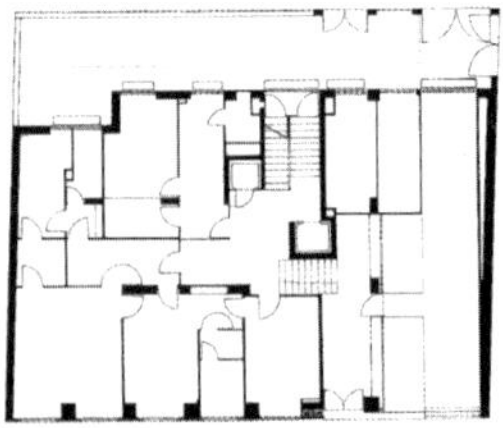

architect
Asnago and Vender

type
residential, offices

construction
1935-1936

25. The Pirelli Skyscraper

Piazza Duca d'Aosta 3
20124 Milan

access by appointment

5
Stazione Centrale -
Piazza Duca d'Aosta

M2/M3
Centrale FS

FS
Centrale

60/81
Stazione Centrale -
Piazza Duca d'Aosta

Placed in what was the emerging Centro Direzionale business centre of Milan at the time, the Pirelli tower was presented by Ponti as emblematic of certain key objectives of his architectural research, beginning with its completed form, its pure essential line, and its structural and representational invention.
With its height of 127 metres, at the moment of construction, the tower was one of the highest in Europe, and served as inspiration for buildings all over the world such as the Pan Am Building in New York (1958-1963) by Emery Roth & Sons, Walter Gropius and Pietro Belluschi. It features an unusual diamond shape tapering towards the ends of the building terminating with a vertical slit the whole height of the structure that sits on a base containing an auditorium. The reinforced concrete structure, the result of clever collaboration between architect and engineer, is composed of vertebrae that cross the main body of the structure and that taper from a width of 2 metres at the base to 50 centimetres on the top floor. Initially designed for the Pirelli company which supplied much of the material used for the internal spaces, the building was purchased by the Lombardy Regional Authority in 1978, and underwent redevelopment work, in particular after 2002, after damage to the twenty-sixth floor following a plane crash into the building.

architect
Gio Ponti, Antonio Fornaroli, Alberto Rosselli, Giuseppe Valtolina, Egidio Dell'Orto with Arturo Danusso and Pier Luigi Nervi

type
offices

construction
1955-1960

26. Milan Central Station

Piazza Duca d'Aosta 1
20124 Milan

open to public

www.milanocentrale.it

5
Stazione Centrale -
Piazza Duca d'Aosta

M2/M3
Centrale FS

FS
Centrale

60/81
Stazione Centrale -
Piazza Duca d'Aosta

Second in Italy for its size and traffic volume, the Central Station in Milan was inaugurated in 1931; the design was based on the winning project in a competition held in 1912. It replaced the previous station situated in Piazza della Repubblica.
This imposing building with its facade over 200 metres long overlooking Piazza Duca d'Aosta and its iron and glass roof over 340 metres long, is an architectural style strongly influenced by the past, by classicism and with a strong monumental impact. The main body of the building was recently restored under the direction of Marco Tamino, based on the reorganisation of intermodal transport access, restructuration of internal travel systems, and the creation of new service and shopping areas.
At street level, today a Shoah Memorial has been erected (2008-2013) designed by Morpurgo and De Curtis on the location of former track 21 where trains left to take deportees towards the concentration camps. It is composed of the Memorial monument, as witness to the tragic events, a Laboratorio della Memoria, (Research and archives) including a Library and an auditorium with a seating capacity for 200.

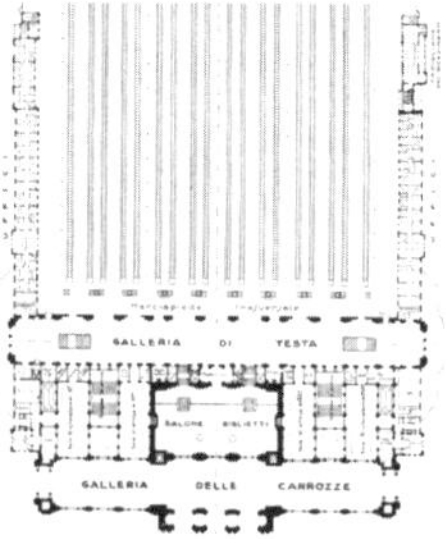

architect
Ulisse Stacchini

type
station

construction
1912-1931

27. Residential Apartments in Piazza Carbonari

Piazza Carbonari 2
20125 Milan

external viewing only

5
Viale Marche -
Piazza Carbonari

M3
Sondrio

The building rises in an isolated area of the northern outskirts of the city and, similar to other examples like those of Via Nievo (1956-1957), Corso Italia (1957-1961), Via Santa Maria alla Porta (1960-1962), Via Santa Croce (1959-1964), Corso Monforte (1963-1966) and Via Catena (1968-1970), it represents an emblematic episode in Caccia Dominioni's research into residential project design.
The shape was determined by the interpretation of building regulations: in particular, the vertical construction was influenced by the necessity to leave at least 450 square metres of the available 1,300 sq. metre plot as green space, and the irregular roof profile had to obey height limits between the front facade towards the piazza and the rear side. The facades clad with ceramic stone tiles reveal a pattern of openings whose variations are due to the diversification of the apartment layouts. Among these openings, the northern side is punctuated by the narrow slot of the elevator shaft, and the convex form of the two-storey bow-window structures that create spatial continuity between the kitchen and dining areas.
The interiors of the apartments are well structured with offset partitions, alcoves, built-in furniture and use of extra space obtained by positioning the window frames on the facade surface.

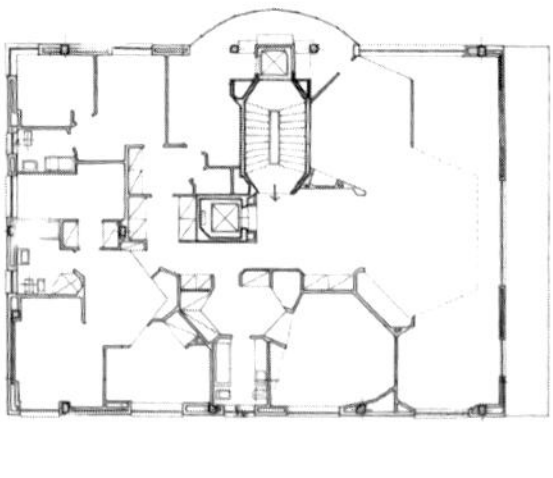

architect
Luigi Caccia Dominioni

type
residential

construction
1960-1961

28. Palazzo Lombardia

Piazza Città di Lombardia 1
20124 Milan

external viewing only

M2
Gioia

60/728
Via Gioia - Via Galvani

The project for Palazzo Lombardia was created to incorporate the offices of the Regione Lombarda (Lombardy Regional Authority) which had been previously located in various buildings around the city; it is composed of three elements: the 43-storey tower 161 metres tall, the seven and eight storey base buildings, and the linear garden areas.
While the plan of the open spaces is based on a Cartesian layout, recalling the irrigation systems in the plains to the south of the city, the organic forms of the buildings evoke the mountain ranges to the north: the complex recalls towering mountains divided by deep valleys and riverbeds crossing the covered open space considered the heart of the complex and opened up to the city for events and performances. Research into environmental sustainability resulted in the use of double skin climatic walls, living green roofs, heating pumps run on groundwater, and solar panels.
Compared to the enclosed, convex single structure of the Pirelli Tower, until now considered the symbolic icon of Milan's skyline, the Palazzo Lombardia aims at a complementary concept, with a dual form, both open and concave.

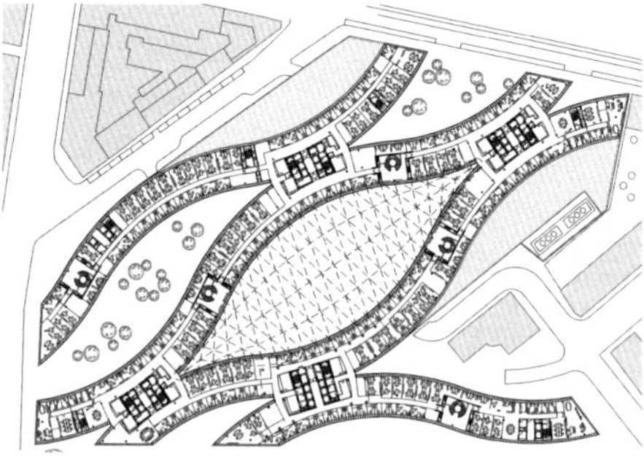

© Pei Cobb Freed & Partners

architect	**type**	**construction**
Pei Cobb Freed & Partners	offices	2004-2013

29. Incubatore dell'Arte

Via Gaetano De Castillia 26
20124 Milan

external viewing only

33
Porta Garibaldi

M2/M5
Garibaldi

FS/S1/S2/S5/S6/S13
Garibaldi

37
Porta Garibaldi

Despite its compact size, about 800 square metres, this small building represents a fundamental element in its social role as part of the redevelopment of the Garibaldi-Isola district, because it is able to house the headquarters of several cultural and artisanal associations some of which were previously present in the industrial buildings of the former Brown Boveri plant.
The "Incubator" is composed of a two-storeyed elongated parallepiped, with expanded aluminium mesh wall coverings and rows of vertical windows that create a dialogue with the new skyline of towers that have been completed or are under construction in the surrounding neighbourhoods. Apart from the reinforced concrete core for the elevator shaft and bathroom facilities, all infill panels, insulation and cladding was dry-mounted and assembled to permit easy future reconfiguration of internal spaces if necessary according to possible changes of activity or use. The roofing, composed of the same expanded metal mesh as the facades, is equipped with photovoltaic and solar panels.

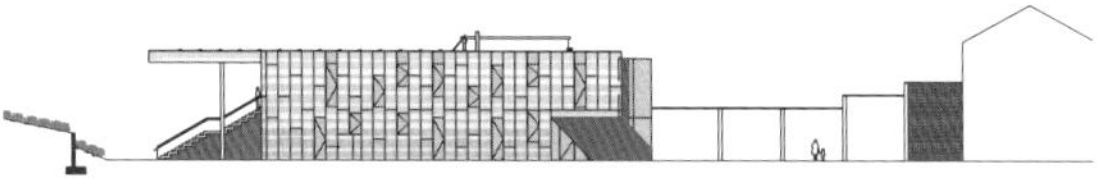

© Boeri Studio

architect
Boeri Studio

type
cultural centre

construction
2010-2011

30. Bosco Verticale (Vertical Forest)

Via Gaetano De Castillia
20124 Milan

external viewing only

www.residenzeportanuova.com/it/residenze-bosco-verticale

33
Porta Garibaldi

M2/M5
Garibaldi

FS/S1/S2/S5/S6/S13
Garibaldi

37
Porta Garibaldi

Bosco Verticale is a complex composed of two residential towers 76 metres (tower D) and 110 metres (Tower E) high, that feature dozens of balconies planted with hanging gardens containing 900 trees and 2000 shrubs and flowering plants.
The tree species, chosen with maximum biodiversity in mind, contribute towards creating a new, more comfortable microclimate. The vegetation absorbs CO^2 and dust particles while simultaneously producing oxygen and providing protection from radiation and acoustic pollution. Each species was painstakingly selected according to its maximum growth potential by studying the continuous bands on the building facades to permit the natural expansion of trees that will reach between 6 and 7.5 metres in height, and the positioning of the terraces, whose plants will remain below 3 metres in height.
The plants will be grown in tubs built to contain the root development, and the climatic conditions of each position have been carefully considered, determined by specific height and exposition, in relation to the sunlight and wind strength.

© Boeri Studio

© Paolo Sacchi

architect
Boeri Studio

type
residential

construction
2007-2013

31. Unicredit Headquarters

Piazza Gae Aulenti
20124 Milan

external viewing only

33
Porta Garibaldi

M2/M5
Garibaldi

FS/S1/S2/S5/S6/S13
Garibaldi

37
Porta Garibaldi

The Unicredit tower, the tallest in Italy, 231 metres to the tip of the spire, represents one of the first projects completed in the Porta Nuova urban redevelopment plan and is composed of three curved buildings (the tallest Tower A is flanked by Tower B, 100 metres tall, and Tower C, 50 metres tall) that enclose a partially covered circular open space (Piazza Aulenti).
The complex rises from a massive podium with underground parking, surrounded by a dual level shopping centre with restaurants; this raised open space can be reached through the entrance from Porta Garibaldi and by escalator from Corso Como. The piazza is accessed from Quartiere Isola on a long gently sloping ramp. The main building structures are built in reinforced concrete, with a curtain wall facade, interrupted horizontally with narrow slatted brise-soleil sun protection. The buildings also feature energy saving elements such as high-performance glass windows, advanced construction technology, and high efficiency lighting.

architect
Pelli Clarke Pelli Architects

type
offices, commercial

construction
2009-2013

32. Porta Nuova Building

Piazza Gae Aulenti,
Via Fratelli Castiglioni
20124 Milan

ground floor access only

33
Porta Garibaldi

M2/M5
Garibaldi

FS/S1/S2/S5/S6/S13
Garibaldi

37
Porta Garibaldi

The elongated curvilinear profile 140 metres long is the feature that distinguishes this building, that assumes a dual aspect because of its unusual position. On one side, the urban facade facing the city centre is screened with full height vertical brise-soleil slatting.
On the larger curved side facing Piazza Aulenti and the new public spaces, the building facade is almost entirely glazed, and contained by a white projecting rim that follows the whole perimeter of the building. This conveys the impression of a large container open on the two longer sides. The 22,500 square metres space houses stores and cafés (at piazza level under a portico structure) and office space on the five upper floors. Inaugurated in 2013, this building was the result of a design competition in 2006, and proposes a high-impact horizontal concept in an area where vertical architecture predominates. The uniform flat roofing is enlivened by a series of openings and overhead lighting into internal courtyards.

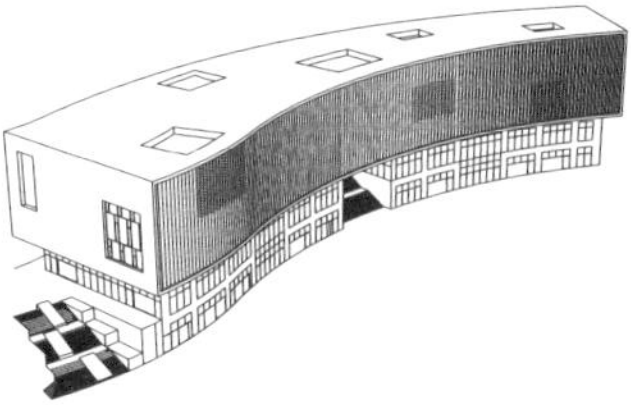

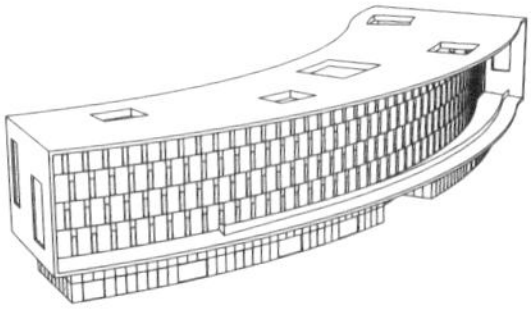

architect
Piuarch

type
offices

construction
2010-2013

33. Public Spaces Porta Nuova Garibaldi, Porta Nuova Varesine, Porta Nuova Isola

Piazza Gae Aulenti,
Piazza Lina Bo Bardi,
Via Gaetano de Castillia
20124 Milan

open to public

33
Porta Garibaldi

M3/M5
Garibaldi

FS/S1/S2/S5/S6/S13
Garibaldi

37
Porta Garibaldi

The project for the public spaces of Porta Nuova connecting the zones of Garibaldi, Varesine and Isola in the largest redevelopment plan in the centre of Milan (290,00 square metres) was created by LAND Milano, which also created the landscaping at New Park at Portello (2012) and Bicocca (1994).
The master plan is based on urban, infrastructural and environmental sustainability, and is designed not simply to create a route connecting the various zones, but also a meeting point for both culture and leisure.
The focal point of the Garibaldi project is the raised piazza (Piazza Gae Aulenti) bordered by the Unicredit office building, with fountains and pools, large oval openings to provide light in the lower level, a 105 metre concrete and marble bench sculpture, and two projecting roofs (the lower to provide shade, the upper layer for solar panels). The route for the Varesine area has a strong pedestrian traffic flow and links the two piazzas (Lina Bo Bardi and Alvar Aalto) with a walkway (Promenade) flanked with hanging gardens; the project for the Isola area is focussed mainly on planted green park areas to create continuity between the existing housing and population and new interventions, with a Piazza Verde (green park) for leisure, and the Giardino dei Ciliegi (cherry garden) to give the neighbourhood a specific identity.

© LAND Milano

architect
LAND Milano srl, Edaw

type
public space

construction
2010-2014

34. Corso Como, Corte Verde Apartment Complex

Via Gaspare Rosales 8
20124 Milan

external viewing only

33
Porta Garibaldi

M2/M5
Garibaldi

FS/S1/S2/S5/S6/S13
Garibaldi

37
Porta Garibaldi

Located in the area of Porta Nuova, in a position of transition between the new high-rise constructions to the north and the existing consolidated districts to the south, this residential complex is spread along the eastern side because of the elongated trapeze shape of the construction lot.
The facade surfaces and distribution layout differ according to the views and sunlight. The east side on Via Viganò features projecting bow-windows and rows of floor to ceiling windows, while the opposite side is composed of continuous irregular balconied terraces and a tiered profile on the upper floor apartments for terrace gardens. The materials employed (plaster, Indian stone in two alternative finishes, porphyry for the base and painted wood and metal for the door and window frames) have been selected to form a harmonised clay-toned colour palette.
The major design reference is the Milanese urban style, not as an echo of stylistic features, but through of a process of new abstract processing and interpretation.

© Cino Zucchi Architetti

architect
Cino Zucchi Architetti

type
residential

construction
2011-2013

35. Diamond Tower

Via della Liberazione,
Via Galileo Galilei
20124 Milan

external viewing only

9
Piazza San Gioachimo

With its complex geometry, this skyscraper (thirty floors of office space 140 metres high) closes the Varesine quarter overlooking Piazza della Repubblica, facing towards the city centre. The Diamond Tower, completed in 2012, owes its name to the faceted angles of a facade that "bends" on the ninth floor on one side of the building, and at the twenty-second floor on the other, hybridizing the verticality normally associated with skyscrapers.

Painstaking research into dynamism and multi-storey construction has resulted in innovative solutions by the structural engineers (Ove Arup): a bearing structure with steel columns (at the time of inauguration - the highest building in Italy using this technology) is positioned along the perimeter around a central reinforced concrete core. The foundation slab is also built of reinforced concrete, over 2 metres thick. Above the four underground levels, the ground floor has a height of nine metres with a footprint of about 30 x 50 metres. This new iconic architectural symbol on the Milan skyline features a continuous and uniform facade finish, with full-height aluminium and glass elements designed to highlight the innovative shape.

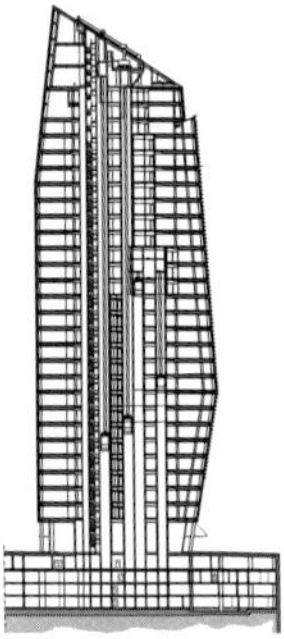

architect
Kohn Pedersen Fox

type
offices

construction
2012-2013

36. Feltrinelli Porta Volta

Viale Pasubio
20154 Milan

open to public

www.feltrinelliportavolta.it

2/4
Viale Montello - Piazzale Baiamonti

S9
Porta Romana

94
Viale Montello - Piazzale Baiamonti

This project is set in an area that has very strong historical links with the city, and is located along the line of the traces of the 15th century Spanish Walls; the new constructions are built just behind two customs houses which are identical in design and acted as a gate into the city, now emphasised by the position and character of the new buildings.
The project foresees the construction of several buildings: the complex for the foundation will house a bookstore and a café on the ground floor, a double-height multi-function space on the first floor, office spaces on the second, and a reading room dedicated to the Giangiacomo Feltrinelli Foundation archives on the top floor. Other floors are destined for offices and meeting areas; the external grounds are landscaped with planted green spaces, cycling and walking paths.
The new buildings whose design is based on repeated structural themes, are inspired by the imposing scale of certain historical Milanese buildings such as the Ca' Granda at the Sforzesco Castle, and by the long linear architecture of traditional Lombardy rural farm buildings.

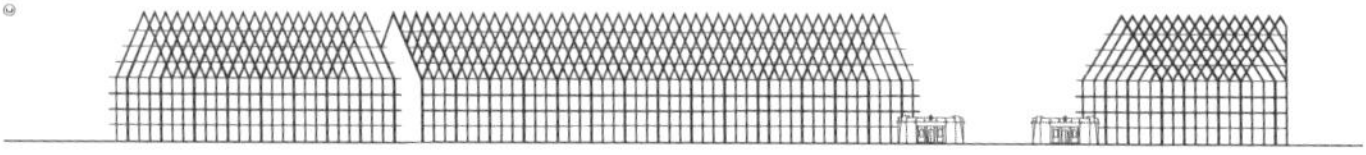

architect
Herzog & de Meuron

type
library, exhibition, lecture hall

construction
2008-2016

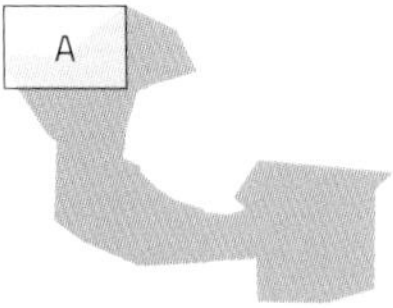

Consolidated urban areas

37. Lomazzo 52 Apartment Buildings
38. Casa Rustici
39. INA Apartment Buildings
40. The Citylife Towers
41. Hadid Apartment Complex
42. Libeskind Apartment Complex
43. Il Sole 24 Ore Headquarters

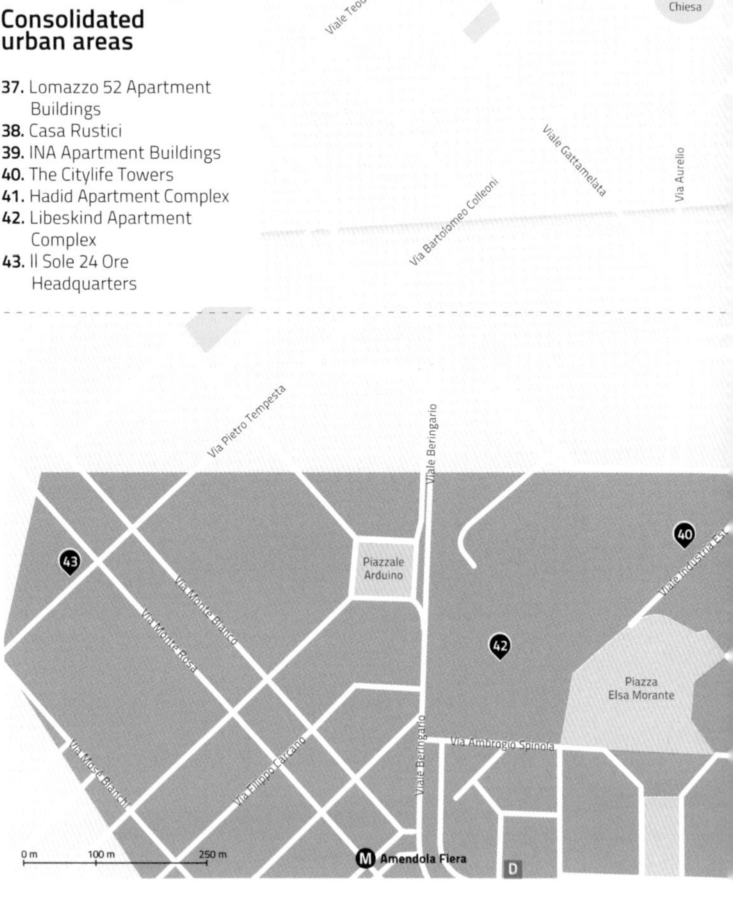

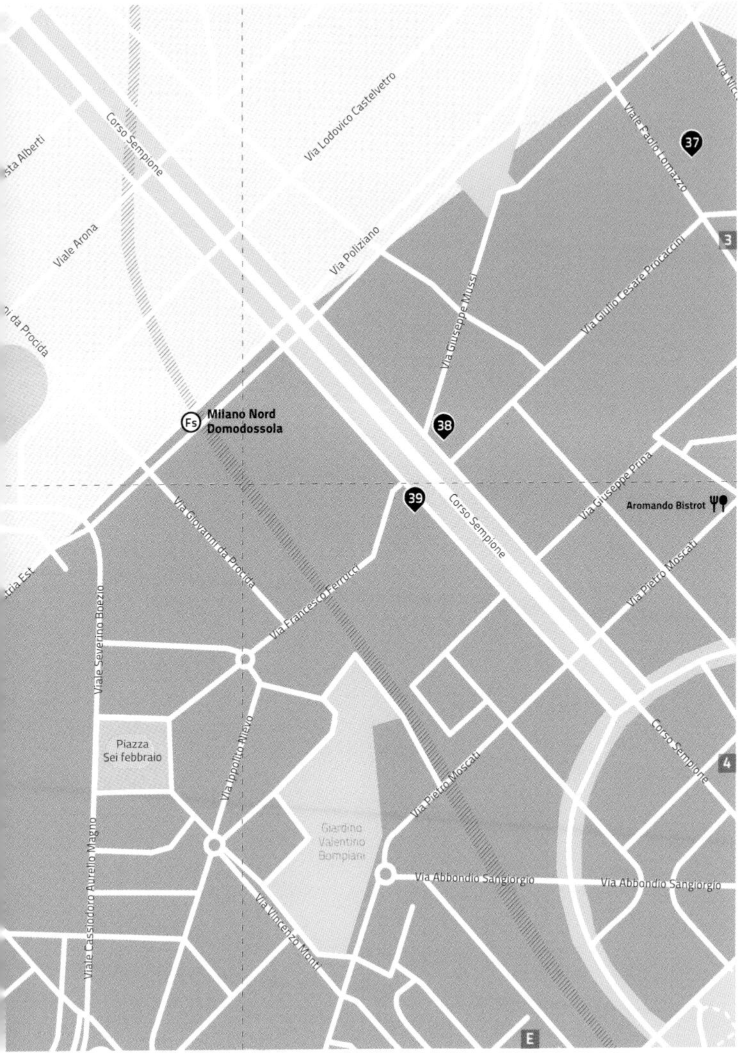
Via Lodovico Castelvetro
Corso Sempione
Viale Arona
Via Poliziano
Viale Paolo Lomazzo
37
3
Via Giuseppe Mussi
Via Giulio Cesare Procaccini
Milano Nord
Domodossola
38
39
Via Giuseppe Prina
Aromando Bistrot
Via Giovanni da Procida
Corso Sempione
Via Pietro Moscati
Via Francesco Ferrucci
Viale Severino Boezio
Piazza
Sei febbraio
Via Ippolito Nievo
Corso Sempione
4
Via Pietro Moscati
Giardino
Valentino
Bompiani
Viale Cassiodoro Aurelio Magno
Via Abbondio Sangiorgio
Via Abbondio Sangiorgio
Via Vincenzo Monti
E

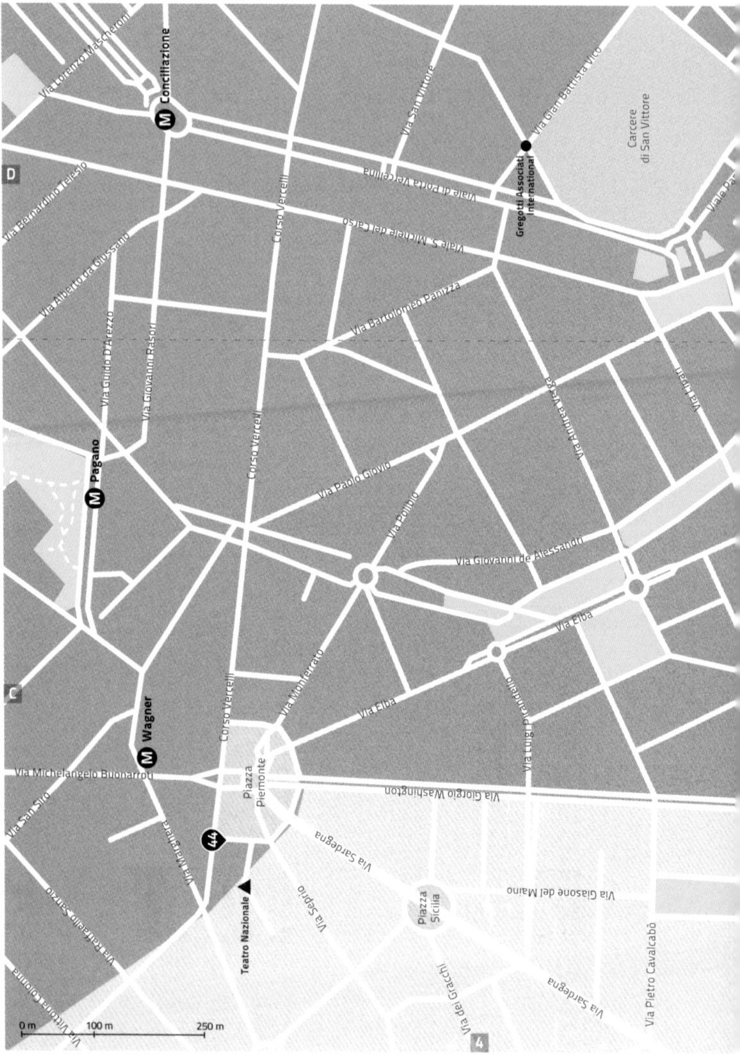

Conciliazione
Via Lorenzo Mascheroni
Via Bernardino Telesio
Via Alberto da Giussano
Via Guido D'Arezzo
Via Giovanni Rasori
Pagano
Corso Vercelli
Via San Vittore
Viale di Porta Vercellina
Viale S. Michele del Carso
Via Gian Battista Vico
Gregotti Associati International
Carcere di San Vittore
Via Bartolomeo Panizza
Via Paolo Giovio
Via Pollaiolo
Via Andrea Verga
Via Giovanni de Alessandri
Via Elba
Via Monferrato
Wagner
Via Michelangelo Buonarroti
Piazza Piemonte
Via Giorgio Washington
Via Luigi Pirandello
Via San Siro
Via Raffaello Sanzio
Via Vittoria Colonna
Via Sardegna
Via Sepio
Teatro Nazionale
44
Piazza Sicilia
Via Giasone del Maino
Via dei Gracchi
Via Pietro Cavalcabò
D
C
4
0 m
100 m
250 m

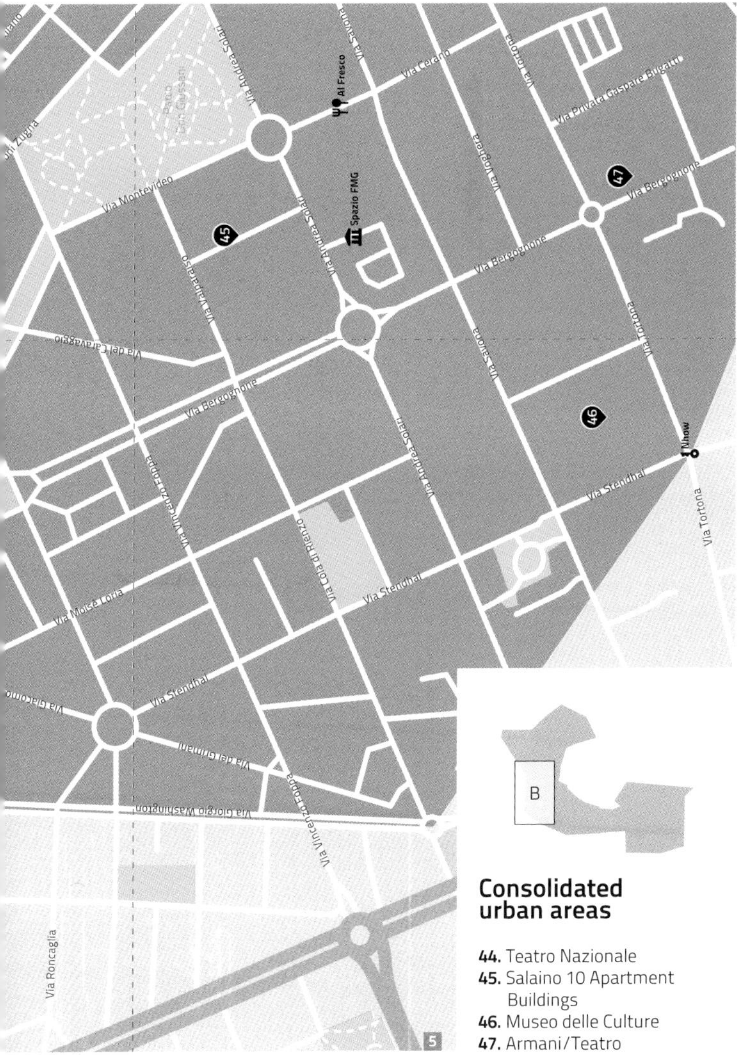

Consolidated urban areas

44. Teatro Nazionale
45. Salaino 10 Apartment Buildings
46. Museo delle Culture
47. Armani/Teatro

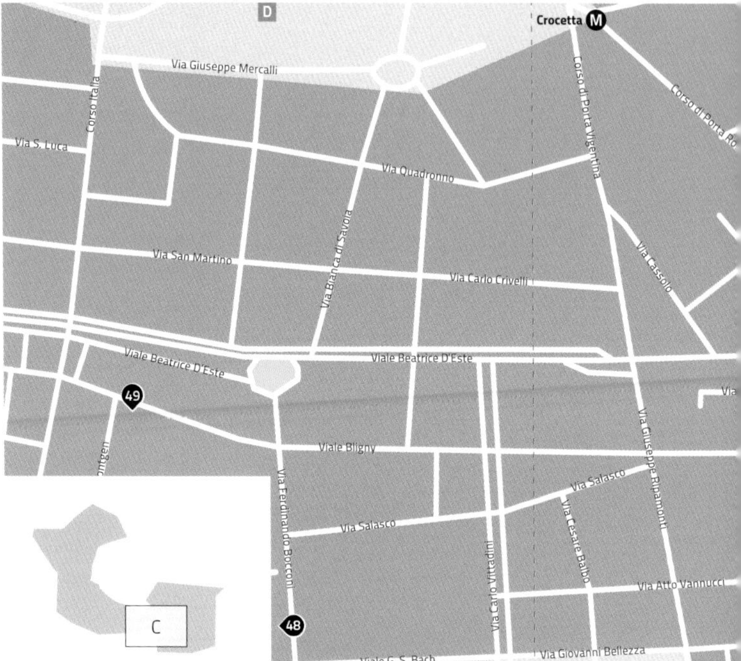

Consolidated urban areas

48. Bocconi University
49. New Aula Magna Auditorium and Department Building at Bocconi University
50. Fondazione Prada
51. Renovation of the Franco Parenti Theatre
52. Apartment Building in Via Maestri Campionesi
53. Renovation of the former Palazzo dei Frigoriferi Milanesi

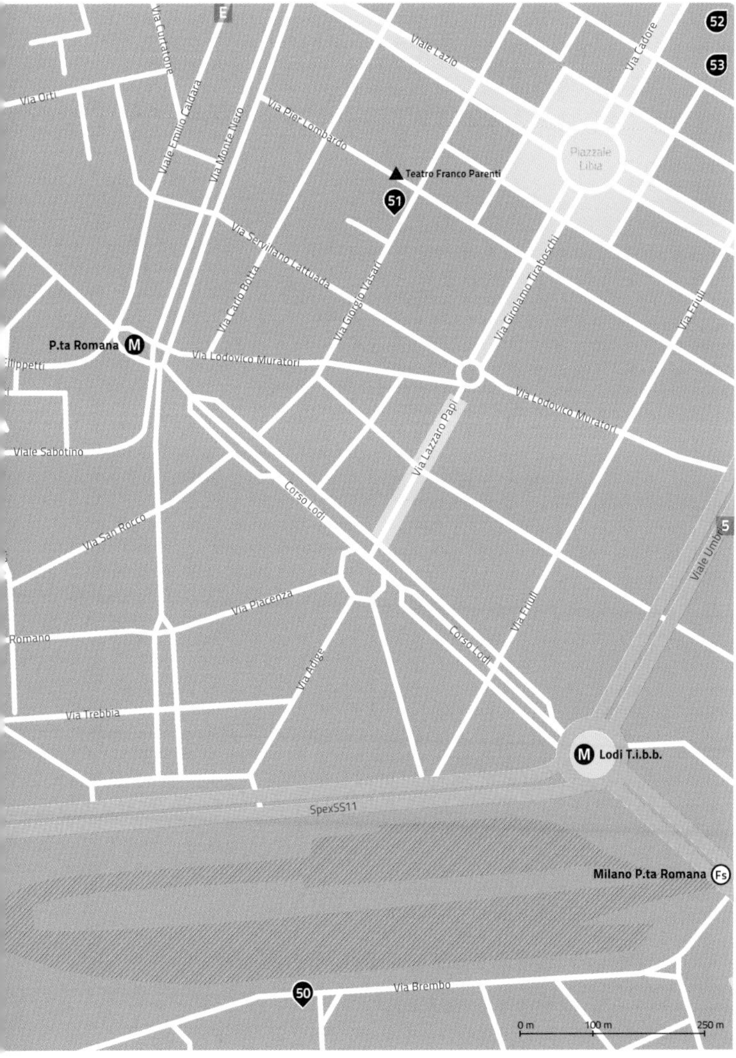
E
Via Curtatone
Viale Lazio
Via Cadore
52
53
Via Orti
Viale Emilio Caldara
Via Monte Nero
Via Pier Lombardo
Piazzale Libia
Teatro Franco Parenti
51
Via Serviliano Lattuada
Via Carlo Botta
Via Giorgio Vasari
Via Girolamo Tiraboschi
Via Friuli
P.ta Romana
Via Lodovico Muratori
Via Lodovico Muratori
Via Lazzaro Papi
Viale Sabotino
Corso Lodi
5
Via San Rocco
Viale Umbria
Via Piacenza
Via Friuli
Corso Lodi
Via Adige
Romano
Via Trebbia
Lodi T.i.b.b.
SpexSS11
Milano P.ta Romana
50
Via Brembo
0 m
100 m
250 m

37. Lomazzo 52 Apartment Buildings

Via Paolo Lomazzo 52
20154 Milan

external viewing only

www.52greenway.it

12
Via Procaccini -
Via Lomazzo

37
Via Procaccini -
Via Lomazzo

The residential building in Via Lomazzo 52 is composed of three structures designed to define the margins and open spaces in a construction lot with an irregular shape. The common structural base forms the connective element of the three buildings.
The wing along the street side houses a floor of duplex apartments, on the northern side is a sixteen-storey tower, and a six-storey building sits on the eastern side. The layout of the three buildings defines the internal trapeze-shaped courtyard space. The architectural style reflects the rational Milanese tradition with elements such as ceppo di Gré stone cladding, regular geometrical layout, and the use of metal trellis, detached from the facade as a decorative feature on the tower and the two upper floors of the eastern wing. The density of the building is balanced by the void of the courtyard that acts as a centre of gravity. The sober elegant base of the wing facing the street with its large openings with wooden frames and ceppo di Gré stone cladding, reflects the style of the adjacent buildings and is suspended above the ground to show a gentle well-ordered internal garden and water feature with its sculptural but domestic tranquillity. This ground floor view is gift to the city, deserved but unexpected.

architects
Antonio Citterio
Patricia Viel and Partners,
Anna Giorgi and Partners

type
residential

construction
2008-2011

38. Casa Rustici

Corso Sempione 36
20145 Milan

external viewing only

1/19
Corso Sempione - Via Procaccini

S3/S4
Domodossola

Compared to the other four complexes built in Milan by Lingeri and Terragni – Case Toninelli (1933-1934), Ghiringhelli (1933-1934), Lavezzari (1934) and Rustici Comolli (1935) – Casa Rustici stands out for the greater complexity of its functional design. The building is composed of two separate elements, set perpendicular to Corso Sempione, each one equipped with its own staircases and elevators. The two buildings are connected by a series of gallery-walkways running along the whole main facade. A basement floor houses technical service areas, offices and garages, and the first floor contains office spaces and the guardian's apartment. The upper floors house the apartments composed of two groups of three units per floor; the two buildings are united by the single-family villa on the top floor thanks to an enclosed walkway that connects the reception and living areas with the bedroom and bathroom wing. In order to take most advantage of the trapeze-shaped plot, an added construction was built perpendicular to the main building on the facade along Via Mussi, and therefore, not perpendicular to the street. The projecting construction contains a living area with triple aspects.
The marble and orange stucco on the facade undeniably underline the typically rationalist layout of the grid structure.

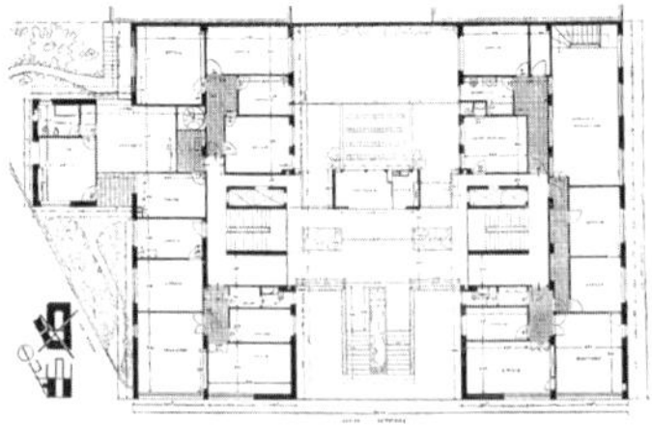

architects
Pietro Lingeri,
Giuseppe Terragni

type
residential

construction
1933-1936

39. INA Apartment Buildings

Corso Sempione 33
20145 Milan

external viewing only

1/19
Corso Sempione -
Via Procaccini

S3/S4
Domodossola

Commissioned by the Istituto Nazionale Assicurazioni, (National Insurance Institute) this tall sharp building recalls the style of the "Milano Verde" plan, drawn up by a group of architects led by Giuseppe Pagano.
At ground level, a porticoed street clad with pink and blue ceramic tiles is punctuated by several shops and access to stairs and elevators; the influence of Le Corbusier can be seen in the idea of creating useable space on the roof and the alternative application for the tenth floor that was to be equipped with hanging gardens and children's playing areas plus some common areas. Un fortunalely, these were suppressed for economic reasons and replaced with other apartment types, but which are recognisably residential thanks to the introduction of covered galleries. The facades featured different aspects: those on the north-west side facing the roads entering the city show the distribution layout based on the juxtaposition of four towers; on the south-west façade the living areas of the apartments face onto a series of open galleries along the whole façade.
The same architect also designed the QT8 Plan (1946-1961), a unique opportunity for experimentation in design and construction for residential projects and public spaces during the period of reconstruction after the war.

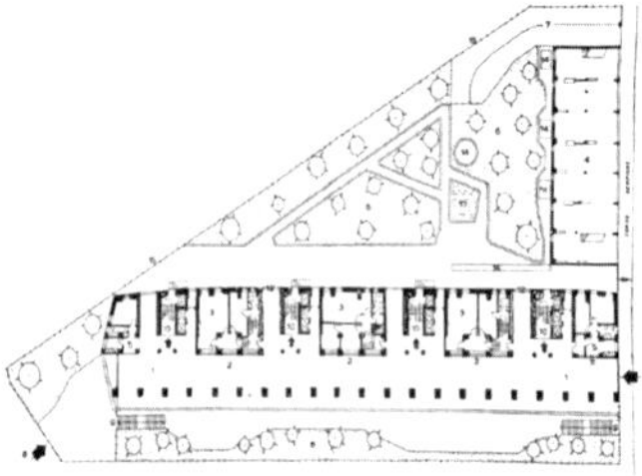

architects
Piero Bottoni

type
residential

construction
1953-1958

40. The Citylife Towers

Viale Industria Est
20145 Milan

external viewing only

www.city-life.it

M1
Amendola Fiera

S3/S4
Domodossola

The Citylife project, promoted by a group of investors guided by Generali Properties with the participation of Allianz Italia, involves the transformation of the area (366,000 sq. metres) which was the site of the previous Milan Trade Fair now rebuilt at the new Rho-Pero exhibition centre; the project will become a new multi-functional business and residential district.
The intervention provided for the creation of three towers in the centre of the plot, each one representative of the architectural language of its designer: Daniel Libeskind with a 153 metre curving skyscraper that recalls a wind-filled sail; Zaha Hadid with a vertical dynamically twisting skyscraper 190 metres high, and Arata Isozaki with his 221 metre skyscraper, the first of the three to be completed in 2015, that is composed of eight convex superimposed modules destined for office space.
The surrounding area is a completely pedestrian zone, and will include a huge park that will become the third largest in Milan after Parco Sempione and the Porta Venezia Gardens; on the other hand, certain projects that had been initially proposed like the Children's Museum and the Contemporary Art Museum by Daniel Libeskind, will not be included.

architects
Daniel Libeskind, Zaha Hadid,
Arata Isozaki + Andrea Maffei

type
offices

construction
2012-2015

41. Hadid Apartment Complex

Via Senofonte,
Viale Cassiodoro
20145 Milan

external viewing only

www.city-life.it

M1
Amendola Fiera

68
Piazzale Giulio Cesare

Composed of seven buildings overlooking two large green internal courtyards inside the CityLife park, the Hadid Residence complex rises on the southern side of the new quarter previously the site of the former Milan fairground. The buildings house a total of 225 apartments and range from five to thirteen storeys, with a profile that creates a sinuous curve against the urban skyline, following the line of the roof terraces on the top floor attic apartments. The fluid profiles of the complex are echoed in the curved balconies, further underlined by the fibre cement facing and natural wood panels on the facades. The buildings are constructed with a triple skin system: aluminium, wood and glass, based on a modular method with different configurations, transparent and opaque, flat and curved, to create a sense of rhythm and fluidity. The double height lobby on the ground floor provides views through the building to the surrounding park areas.

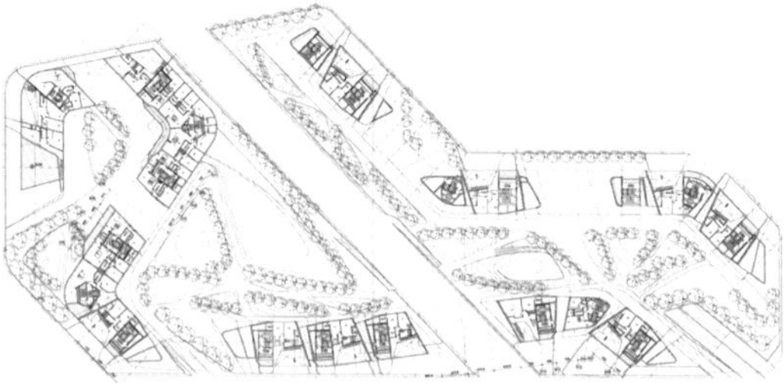

architects
Zaha Hadid Architects,
Marco Piva

type
residential

construction
2009-2013

42. Libeskind Apartment Complex

Via Ambrogio Spinola,
Viale Berengario
20149 Milan

external viewing only

www.city-life.it

M1
Amendola Fiera

68
Amendola Fiera M1

The residential zone designed by Libeskind is composed of eight buildings (five have been completed and three will be finished by 2017) with heights that vary between four and thirteen storeys and with a total of 380 apartment units. The group is part of the elegant CityLife complex, between Piazza Giulio Cesare and Piazza Amendola. Facing the north, the buildings overlook the new public park with panoramic views of the Alps, while the views towards the south face the historical city centre.
Libeskind has interpreted the traditional configuration of the old courtyard housing of Milan proposing buildings that curve gently around a common space, conceived as a relaxing area guaranteeing residents tranquillity and peace of mind. The facades are cladded with a fine weave of pale grey tiles and the fluid line of the highly eco-sustainable irregular wooden brise-soleil structures create a dynamic effect on the external walls.
Double-height attic apartments designed like individual houses are set on the top of each building. These are authentic sky villas featuring a range of different geometrical configurations, large terraces, luxury finishes and extraordinary views over the city.

architects
Daniel Libeskind,
Marco Piva

type
residential

construction
2010-2013

43. Il Sole 24 Ore Headquarters

Via Monte Rosa 91
20149 Milan

external viewing only

M1
Lotto Fiera

49
Lotto Fiera M1

The project for the Milan headquarters of Il Sole 24 Ore newspaper began with the redevelopment and extension of an existing industrial building located between Viale Monte Rosa and Via Tempesta.
Renzo Piano's desire was to construct a building that was "tuned in"; like a newspaper whose headquarters must above all listen to and communicate with its readers, the building must also be tuned in to the city and communicate with it and its population. The notions of transparency, lightness, and technological research are the key concepts of this project. The main body of the building, around an open rectangular courtyard, has a transparent glass facade facing Via Monte Rosa, so that the public can see inside the building, while the facade on Viale Migliara is completely open towards the city. A green hill (an authentic wave 13 metres high) has been created inside the courtyard to offer Milan a new urban park; underneath the hill is an underground auditorium, parking space and technical service areas.

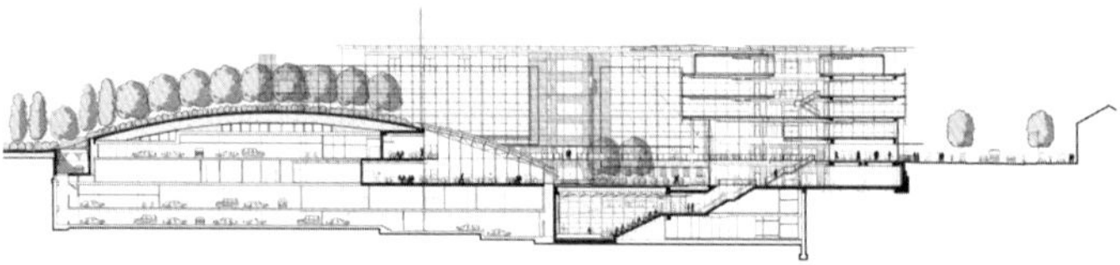

architects
Renzo Piano Building Workshop, architects

type
offices

construction
1998-2005

44. Teatro Nazionale

Via Giordano Rota 1
20145 Milan

open to public

www.teatronazionale.it

16
Piazza Piemonte

67
Piazza Piemonte

Founded by Mauro Rota and inaugurated in 1924 to diffuse theatrical culture beyond the "City centre", the building in Piazza Piemonte was the point of reference in Milan society for operetta, musical revues, and musical comedies, except for a short period during the 1970s when it housed a movie theatre. After a long series of vicissitudes, the building was entrusted to the architect Piero Lissoni, for restructuration in order to give the theatre a new identity for the inauguration in 2009.
The Neo-classical style facade, with its new parvis in Piazza Piemonte, and the main body of the building have remained unaltered, while the sides of the theatre on Via Asti and Via Cuneo have been renewed with an elegant contemporary finish that echoes the colours of the interior, following total refurbishment. With seating for 1,500, the theatre has a stage measuring 14x19 and 21 metres in height, obtained by excavating 5 metres below ground. Rapid scene change systems and excellent acoustic technology complete the new interior finished with dark blue wall panelling. Sculptures by Sassu and Fiume give visual impact in the green space in front of the theatre, part of the Parco delle Arti.

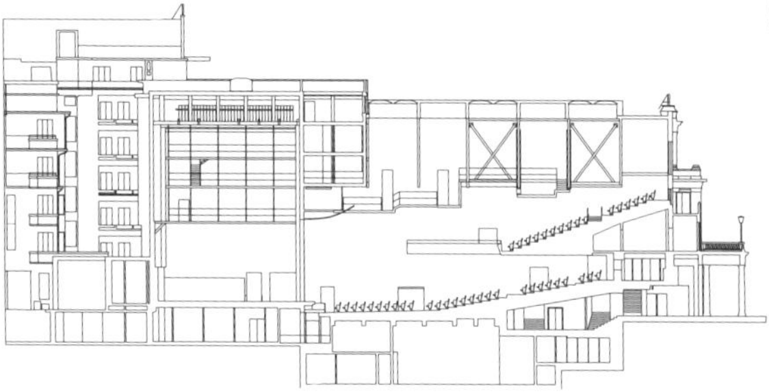

© Lissoni Associati

architects
Lissoni Associati

type
theatre

construction
2009

45. Salaino 10 Apartment Buildings

Via Andrea Salaino 10
20144 Milan

external viewing only

14
Via Montevideo

68
Piazza del Rosario

This project foresaw the urban redevelopment of the area and the conversion for residential use by creating a single rectangular volume (with eight storeys above ground, plus an attic and basement floor) set back from the street but aligned in height with the existing buildings in Via Solari and Via Valparaiso.
The entrance was maintained in Via Salaino 10, with a low loft-style building that recalls the shape of the former construction and provides space for vehicle access to an underground garage and pedestrian flow under a protective portico. The profile is characterised by a sequence of horizontal recesses and each floor has been moved sideways in order to introduce a series of balcony terraces containing tubs planted with small trees. The facades feature an irregular pattern of gilded bronze screen-printed glass panels and a long continuous balcony running along the whole external perimeter.

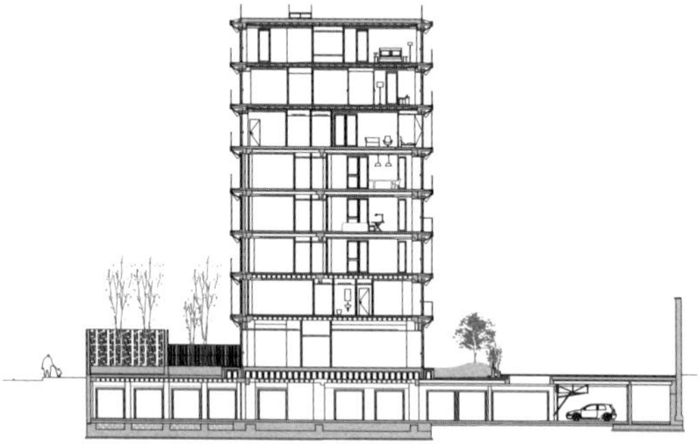

architects
Antonio Citterio
Patricia Viel and Partners

type
residential

construction
2009-2011

46. Museo delle Culture

Via Tortona 56
20144 Milan

open to public

www.mudec.it

2
M2 Porta Genova

M2
Porta Genova

68
Via Bergognone

The Museo delle Culture was constructed on the site of the previous Ansaldi plant, now an urban block located in the Via Tortona district, hub of fashion and design. The project was designed by David Chipperfield, winner of the competition by invitation launched in 1999 for the renovation of the decommissioned industrial area. The project was aimed at maintaining the character enclosed within the plot, separated and hidden from the street by the existing industrial plant walls, with a series of cubic structures clad in titanium-zinc panels to recall the industrial history of the area. To break up the rigid regularity of the layout and define the new function of the project, a curving organic opaque glass structure was set in the centre; the ground floor forms a covered piazza for public and administrative purposes, while the first floor follows the curving circuit of the exhibition spaces. These rooms are grouped in sections according to the hierarchical dimension of the order of the exhibition, in line with general or particular themes, guaranteeing flexibility within the space thanks to selective partitioning systems for the various spaces. At the conclusion of the works, a controversy arose between the designer and the administration concerning certain works on site and the timeframe for construction.

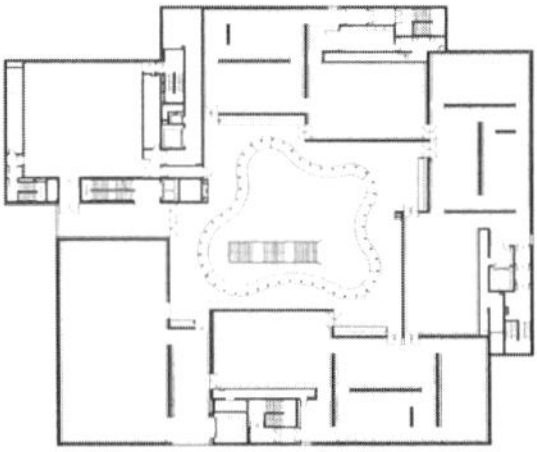

architects
David Chipperfield Architects

type
museum

construction
2008-2015

47. Armani/Teatro

Via Ambrogio da Fossano Bergognone 59
20144 Milan

open to the public only during specific events

M2
Porta Genova

68
Via Bergognone

The project design of this theatre, mainly conceived as a stage for fashion shows, and built to cater to a range of different activities from art to music, represents one of the first examples of ex-industrial building redevelopment in the Ticinese Quarter.
The building is accessed through a passage 100 metres long, punctuated by the regular repetition of square columns set on a slight incline; it leads to a foyer enclosed by a huge sloping curved concrete wall that opens up to the theatre and banquet hall. The space is defined by a range of individual surface finishes separated by beams of light and differentiated by alternating materials that range from pietra serena stone floorings to exposed concrete columns and walls.
The theatre (seating capacity, 558) features a very flexible design that can be adapted for a wide range of events (fashion shows, conferences, art exhibitions) thanks to the removable tiered seating. The banquet hall, which can seat 500 guests, overlooks a 250 square metre pool, enclosed by low windows.

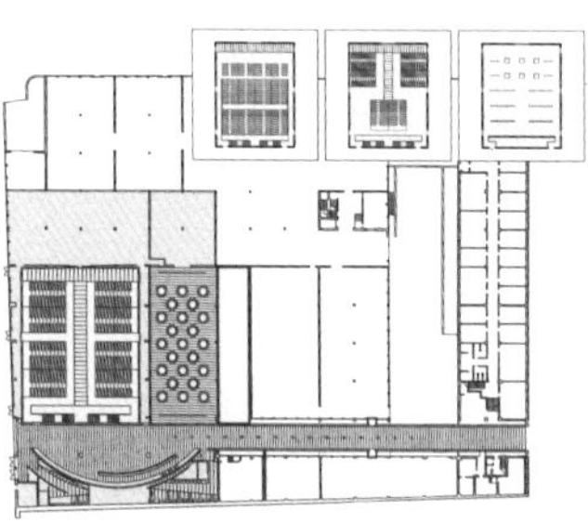

© Tadao Ando Architect & Associates

architect
Tadao Ando

type
mixed-use building

construction
2000-2001

48. Bocconi University

Via Sarfatti, Via Bocconi, Via Gobbi, Via Toniolo
20136 Milan

open to public

www.unibocconi.it

59/79
Via Sarfatti - Via Bocconi

The Bocconi University was built by Ferdinando Bocconi in memory of his son Luigi killed in 1896 at the battle of Adua; it is composed of a series of buildings constructed in several stages.
The original seat of the university was inaugurated in 1902 in Largo Treves, and was later transferred to its current location, when the project design was assigned to Giuseppe Pagano after the project drawn up by the Municipality was abandoned. The design recalls that of the Bauhaus headquarters by Walter Gropius at Dessau (1925-1926) because of the innovative nature of certain choices, in particular the cross-shaped footprint and centrifugal layout, as well as the difference in aspect and dimension in each part of the complex, (the office spaces to the south, the lecture theatres and amphitheatre to the north, service block to the east and other classrooms to the west) according to their particular functions.
Successive interventions were carried out by Giovanni Muzio, first with the student quarters and cafeteria (1956), the second with the new seat in Via Sarfatti (1962-1964) containing the Aula Magna with a capacity for 600, the Library and several other institutes. Alongside the new intervention by Grafton Architects, is the "Velodromo" (1990-2001) by Ignazio and Jacopo Gardella, a four storeyed oval shaped building that features a large central foyer open to full building height.

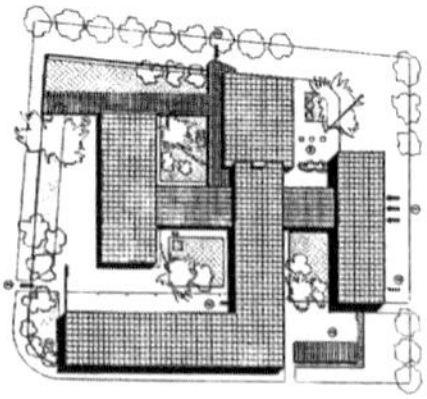

© Matteo Moscatelli

architects
Giuseppe Pagano,
Giovanni Muzio,
Ignazio and Jacopo Gardella

type
university, auditorium,
offices, residential

construction
1937-1941,
1956, 1962-1964,
1990-2001

49. New Aula Magna Auditorium and Department Building at Bocconi University

Via Guglielmo
Corrado Röntgen 1
20136 Milan

open to public

www.unibocconi.it

15
Via Castelbarco

9/59/79
Viale Bligny - Porta Lodovica

This complex was created based on the winning design of a contest held in 2001. It is composed of three buildings: the entrance building in Via Röntgen, the department building in the centre of the block, and the new auditorium in Viale Bligny, with seating for 600 on the lower level and for another 400 on the upper level.
The aim of the project: "to create and defy gravity" resulted in a structural system composed of a sequence of reinforced concrete wall-beams that support the roof from which the office floors are suspended. The main body of the building, conceived like a Broletto or market place, was an experiment to provide the maximum flow between interior and exterior, where the walkways, courtyards and gardens can expand or contract according to the rhythm of the seasons.
As well as the exposed concrete structures, the other surfaces are composed of transparent glass (such as the corner of Viale Bligny and Via Röntgen), opaque glass (for the department facades) and to strengthen the links with Milan, slabs of ceppo di Gré stone of varying thickness.

© grafton architects

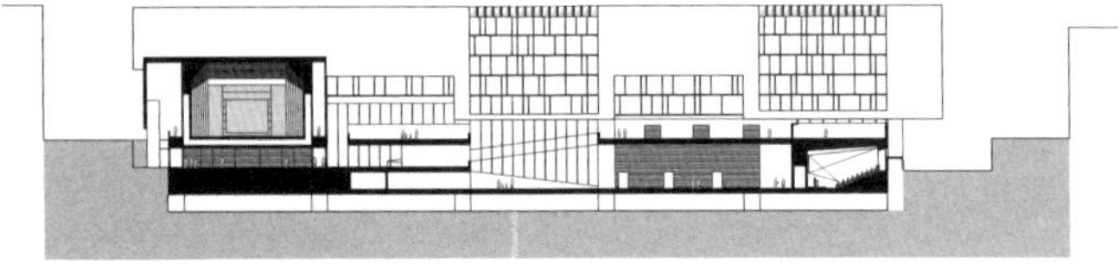

architects
Grafton Architects

type
university,
auditorium, offices

construction
2004-2008

50. Fondazione Prada

Largo Isarco 2
20139 Milan

open to public

www.fondazioneprada.org

M3
Lodi T.i.b.b.

65
Largo Isarco

The new Fondazione complex was created with the transformation of a former distillery dating back to 1910. It is composed of several restored pre-existing buildings, as well as three new constructions: the Podium, Cinema, and Torre.

This private intervention project has been able to offer the city a new centre to increase the understanding and development of contemporary art. It has been designed to offer options with great spatial flexibility and functional versatility: the Great Hall is a cross between an exhibition space and a storage warehouse; alongside is the Torre (still under completion), that will be designed to assume different architectural configurations coherent with the needs of the artists and curators. In the centre of the courtyard sits the Podium, a large open space dedicated to temporary exhibitions, and the Cinema, for use as an events area or as additional gallery space. On the southern side is the "Casa stregata" (Haunted House), a vertical structure with rooms that can be rearranged according to each event. The Prada Archive and Luna Rossa buildings on the northern and eastern sides now house the new bookshop, bar and restaurant spaces. A vast range of different materials has been used to provide an unprecedented combination of surfaces clad in gold leaf and aluminium foam, mirrored facades and polycarbonate partitioning.

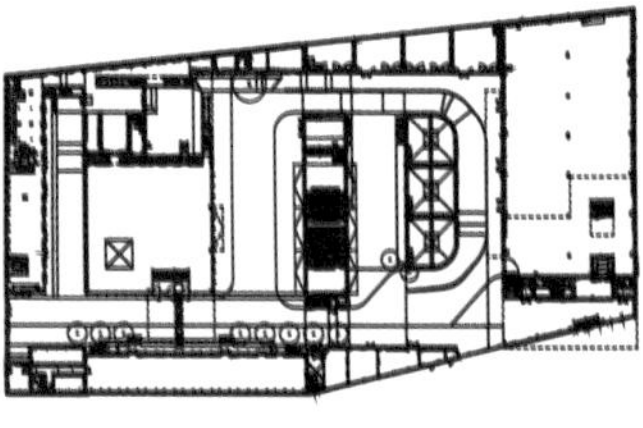

© OMA

Photograph by Bas Princen. Courtesy of Fondazione Prada

architects
OMA

type
exhibition space, auditorium, workshops, offices

construction
2008-2015

51. Renovation of the Franco Parenti Theatre

Via Pier Lombardo 14
20135 Milan

open to public

www.teatrofrancoparenti.it

9
Viale Monte Nero -
Via Pier Lombardo

M3
Porta Romana

This project involves the renovation of the theatre that has had a long-standing tradition in Milan for independent and experimental theatre. The project is focussed on creating a flexible space that can accommodate the wide range of diverse programs proposed by artistic director Andrée Ruth Shammah.
The Sala Grande, at the centre of the complex, has been equipped with a range of mobile platforms that can be combined in various configurations for different uses. The entrance area is designed on two levels: the higher foyer, with its row of windows overlooking the Caimi swimming pool is linked with a terrace and the smaller rooms alongside the Sala Grande; the lower foyer gives access to the Sala delle Colonne (AcomeA), the café-restaurant and the internal courtyards, and when opened up to Sala Grande, can be used as a theatre stage, work space, meeting place and dining area.
The continuous effect through the various spaces is accentuated by the use of the materials such as raw pine for the stage floor and platforms and the fumed oak wood for the mobile steps and permanent tiered seating.

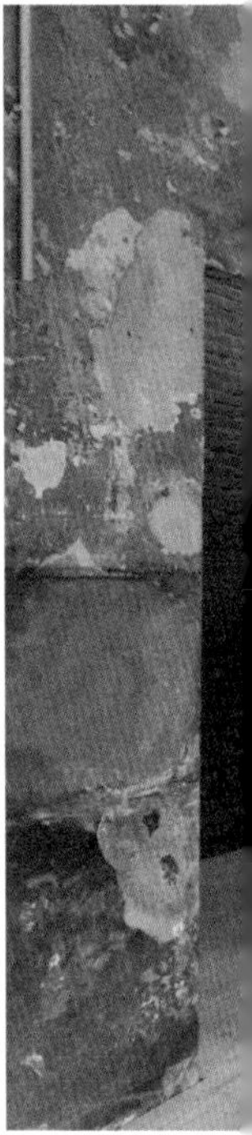

© aMDL

© Mario Carrieri

architects
Michele De Lucchi

type
theatre

construction
2004-2008

52. Apartment Building in Via Maestri Campionesi

Via Maestri Campionesi 15
20135 Milan

external viewing only

84
Via Cadore -
Via Spartaco

Built alongside two pre-existent buildings this residential intervention deals with the recurring problem in Italian cities of replacing old buildings in urban centres.
The building is composed of a total of eight floors above ground and three below ground. The ground floor includes the pedestrian and vehicle entrance and, with the underground basement floors, the common service areas, entrances, personal storage spaces and garages. The ground floor facade is compact and divided into two sections: one solid in the colour and material of the horizontal strips above, and one void, in shade and recessed from the street, repeating the gold-cream colour palette of the upper floor balconies. The complex houses apartments of various sizes from the first floor, including duplex apartments and attic lofts on the sixth and seventh floors.
An unusual aspect of the construction is the layout of the facade; the elements are developed in a three-dimensional sequence, composed of horizontal bands to define each floor, alternating with the vertical fiberglass elements in various shapes and colours, mounted in a staggered arrangement on each floor projecting out and facing different directions to create framed views of the urban landscape.

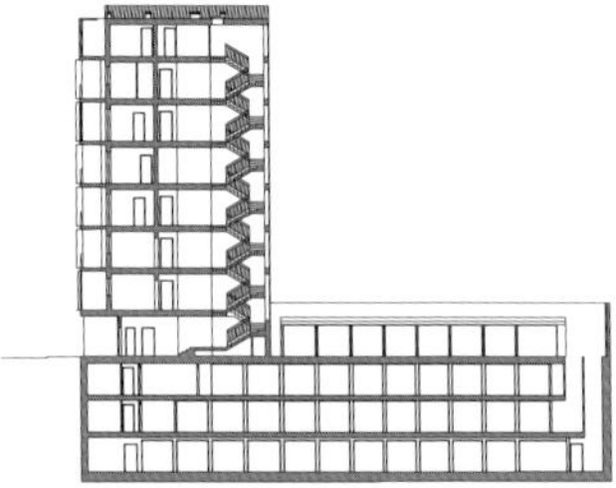

© Archea Associati

architects
Archea Associati

type
residential

construction
2009-2012

53. Renovation of the former Palazzo dei Frigoriferi Milanesi

Via Giovanni Battista Piranesi 10
20137 Milan

open to public

www.frigoriferimilanesi.it

27
Viale Campania - Viale Corsica

S1/S2/S5/S6/S13
Porta Vittoria

45/73
Viale Campania - Viale Corsica

The Frigoriferi Milanesi is a historical industrial complex established in 1899 to house the ice production and cold storage cells of Milan. Another part of the complex was the ice skating rink, the Palazzo del Ghiaccio, a magnificent Art Nouveau style building constructed in 1923. After a long and complicated renovation process, the entire complex has been redeveloped and transformed into a "large cultural centre" with an innovative design, able to house exhibitions, events, performances and concerts. The project "rediscovered the existing volumes" transforming them from inward-looking, enclosed spaces to open buildings that communicate with the city. The massive exterior has been painted black in contrast with the dazzling white interior. The layout has been re-arranged with the help of a series of glass elevators.
Via Piranesi, a street recognised for its closed compact facades, now boasts a long (100 metres) low "slab" coated in glowing red glass in stark contrast with the matt black of the building behind it. The vibrant colour creates a welcoming element that identifies and emphasises the entrance to the entire complex.

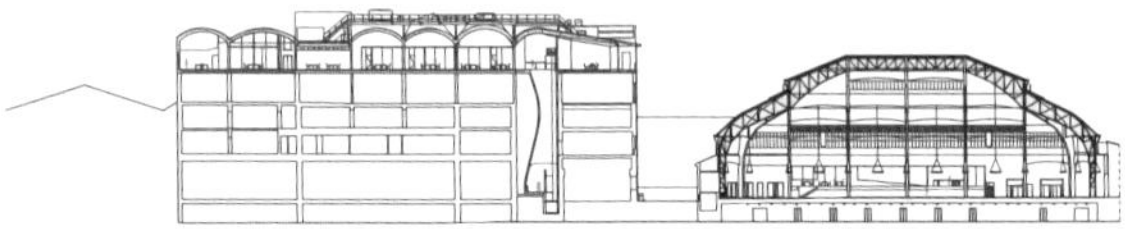

architects
5+1AA

type
exhibition,
restaurant, offices

construction
2003-2008

Greater Milan - North East

54. 3M Headquarters
55. Mondadori Headquarters
56. "Living in Milan" project – Via Civitavecchia
57. RCS Headquarters
58. Church of the Resurrection of Jesus
59. New Campari Central Headquarters

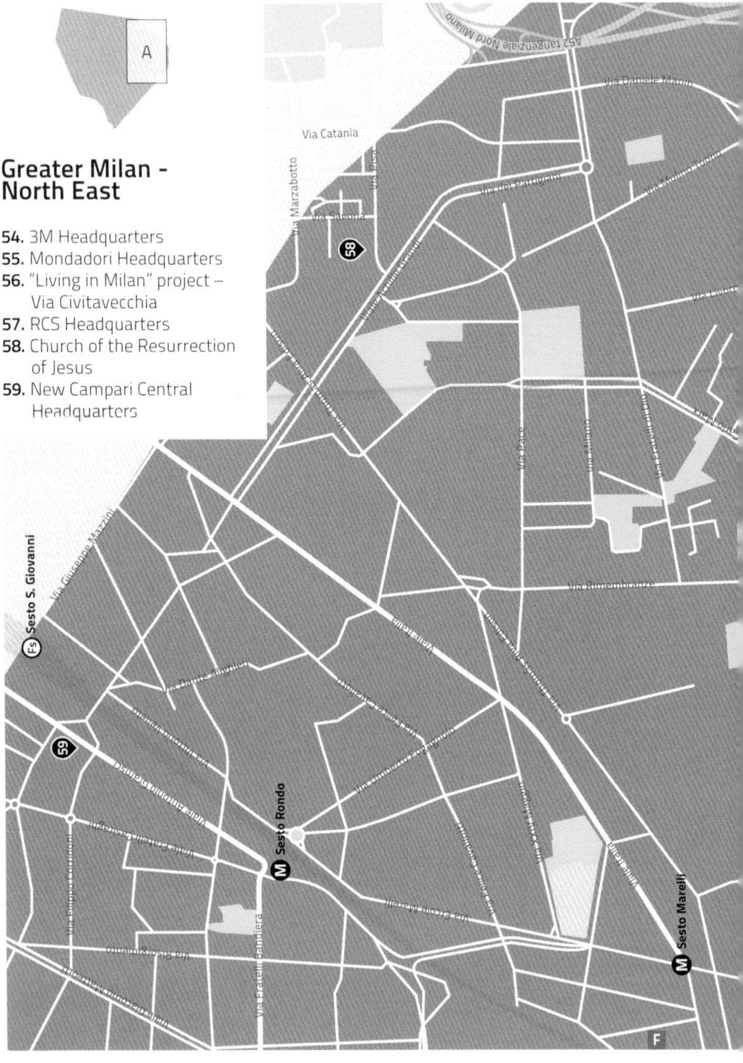

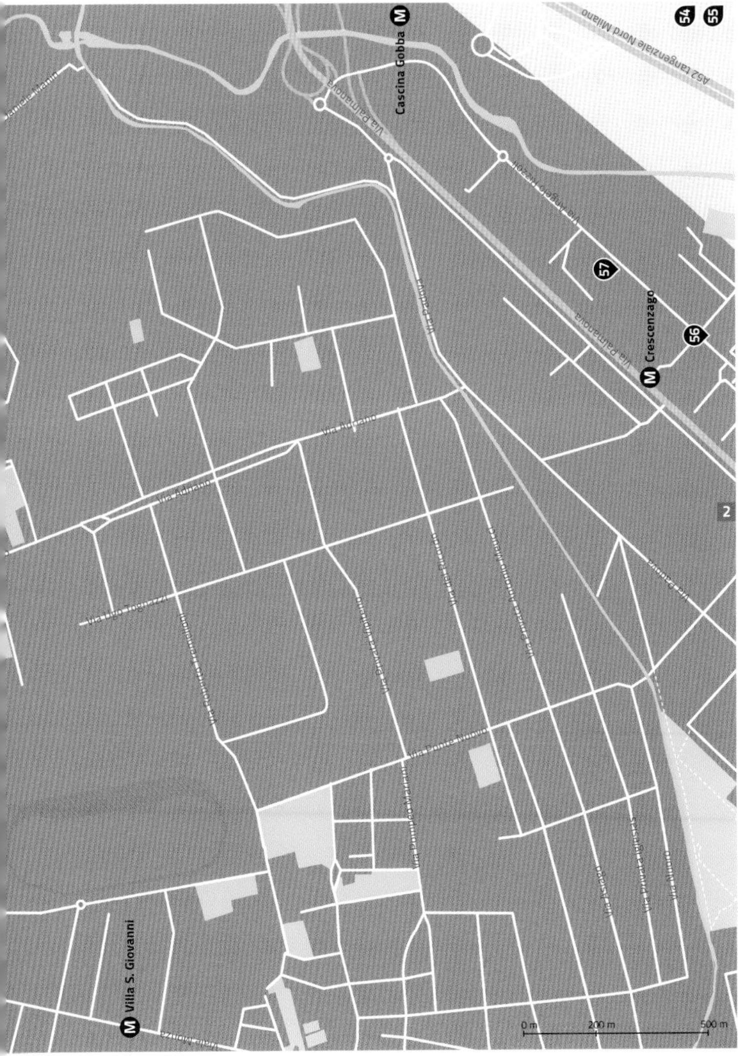
Cascina Gobba
Crescenzago
Villa S. Giovanni
A52 tangenziale Nord Milano
Via Palmanova
Via Padova
Via Adriano
Via Ugo Tognazzi
Via Angelo Rizzoli
Via Ponte Nuovo
Viale Monza
Via Asiago
54
55
56
57
2
0 m
200 m
500 m

D
66
65
Parco Nord Milano
Via Luigi Ornato
Affori Centro
Viale Enrico Fermi
Ospedale Niguarda Ca' Granda
Via Renato Donatelli
Via Carlo Girola
2
Via Pellegrino Rossi
Via Ca' Granda
Via Michele De Angelis
Via Padre Luigi Monti
Dergano
Via Carlo Imbonati
64
Via Gioacchino Murat
Istria
63
Via Monte S. Genesio
Via Valassina
Viale Zara
Maciachini
3
Viale Marche
Marche
Via Francesco Nava
Lancetti
0 m
200 m
500 m

Greater Milan - North East

60. Redevelopment of the Bicocca Area and the Teatro degli Arcimboldi
61. Deutsche Bank
62. Residential home in the Villaggio dei Giornalisti
63. MAC 5-6-7
64. MAC 9 - Zurich Headquarters
65. "Living in Milan" project – Via Senigallia
66. Bi - La Fabbrica del Gioco e delle Arti

54. 3M Headquarters

Via Norberto Bobbio 21
20096 Pioltello

external viewing only

S5/S6

923
Strada Rivoltana -
Via San Bovio

This building is the first element constructed for the master plan project: it was designed for the management headquarters drawn up in 2005 for the Malaspina business park. The building is a dynamic construction, 105 metres long, featuring a shading system composed of painted aluminium brise-soleil slats and a sequence of sloping terraces on the south side that act as an environmental buffer against weather change. The structure is arranged in a series of rectangular buildings: the central building houses the office spaces and vertical elements separated by green internal courtyards; the side building houses common areas and workspaces, while the cafeteria and bar are in the lowest part. The project was designed to respect the maximum environmental sustainability possible with the use of eco-compatible materials, innovative equipment technology and specific choices in form and orientation.

© MCA Archive

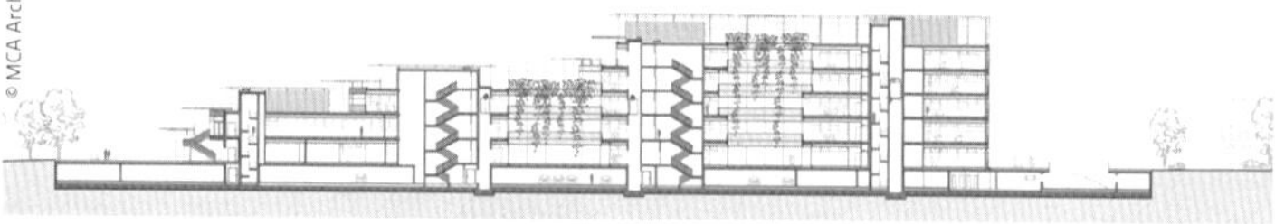

architects
Mario Cucinella
Architects

type
offices

construction
2005-2010

55. Mondadori Headquarters

Via Arnoldo Mondadori 1
20090 Segrate

external viewing only

73/901/923
Strada Rivoltana - Via Buozzi

Located in an isolated area in the landscape to the east of the Idroscalo Park, the complex was built to replace the previous offices in Via Bianca di Savoia, as the city centre location did not permit any extension work.
After rejecting an initial plan composed of two curved structures, it was decided to opt for a solution based on a main structure in a regular rectangular form, intersected by two low organically shaped structures and featuring a series of parabolic arches in reinforced concrete supporting a roof from which was suspended the glassed prism of the office spaces. The project was inspired by the Itamaraty building in Brasilia (1962-1964) by Niemeyer, whose work Giorgio Mondadori had admired while travelling in South America in 1967. The Mondadori building echoes the volumetric configuration; high-precision spacing of the open spaces and the introduction of large reflecting pools, but differs in the spacing between the pillars, which is irregular in the Mondadori building.
The complex was completed with the landscaping project (190.000 square metres) by Pietro Porcinai, the sculpture "Colonna dai grandi fogli" (Column of Great Sheets) by Arnaldo Pomodoro, and the restoration of Cascina Tregarezzo (2005-2010), restored and extended by Werner Tscholl to create a large new courtyard area.

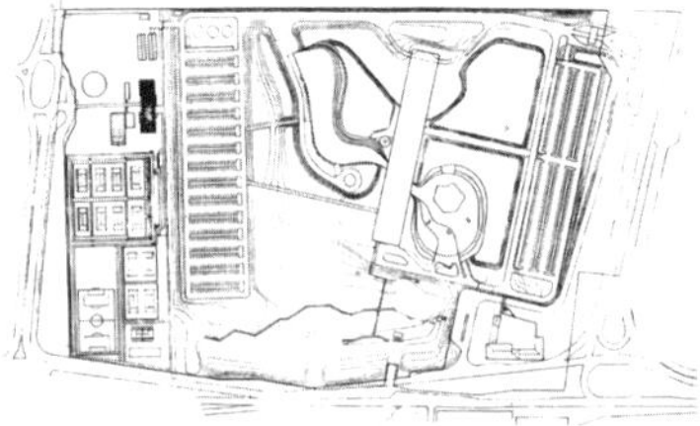

architects
Oscar Niemeyer

type
offices

construction
1968-1975

56. "Living in Milan" project – Via Civitavecchia

Via Civitavecchia,
Via Carlo Cazzaniga
20132 Milan

external viewing only

M2
Crescenzago

75
Crescenzago M2

Located right next to the new RCS media group headquarters, this project is an experiment to link town and country, acting as a connecting element between the Crescenzago district on the outskirts of Milan and the natural environment of the Lambro Park.
The complex is a study in two architectural types: the tower designed as an urban landmark, is composed of a sculptural style block, clad with dark fibrocement panels and punctuated by a series of vertical openings of different sizes; the three linear buildings, located along the route towards the park, but in staggered positions in relation to one another, feature modular housing units that can be combined to create double or triple height recessed terrace spaces on the façade.
The core feature of the complex is the organisation of the common areas, located not only at the base of each building (with guardian's lodge, bicycle storage garage and meeting room) but also on different floors and on the roof where a large roof terrace is equipped with outdoor seating, hanging gardens, and a play area for children enclosed with metal mesh covered with climbing plants.

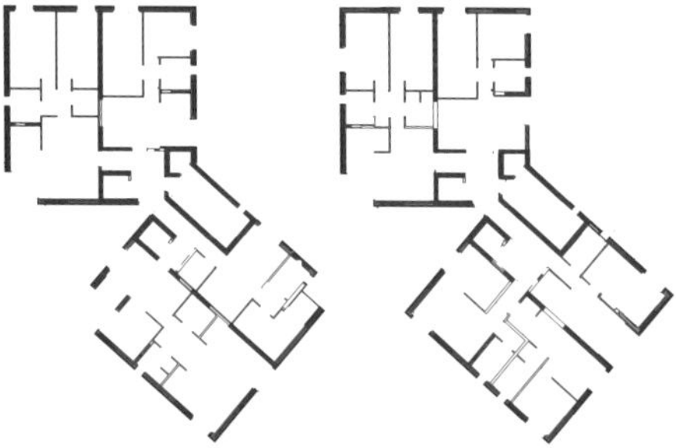

architects
Consalez Rossi
Architetti Associati

type
residential

construction
2006-2010

57. RCS Headquarters

Via Angelo Rizzoli 8
20132 Milan

external viewing only

M2
Crescenzago

75
Via Rizzoli

This project, winner of an international contest launched in 2001, is composed of a parcelling plan for the whole RCS area, and has been designed for construction in several stages.
The core of the complex is Corpo C (Boeri Studio), composed of a low five-storey building plus a nineteen floor tower, 80 metres high. The lower building is constructed completely in reinforced concrete with a blend of materials used for the tower. A framework of steel beams and columns is connected to a concrete core; modular metal panel cladding is applied to the exterior walls with an external skin of glass sheets, spaced with aluminium supports and colour contrast; alternating screen-printed layers give the façade a vibrating effect according to the angle and intensity of the sunlight. The lower floor cladding is Acryterm, an artificial stone attached with invisible fastening systems. The stone slabs are the same size as the glass sheets. Completing the project is Corpo B5 (Barreca & La Varra), with its facade in alternating black and white elements. This building houses the editorial section, photography studios, and the multimedia departments. The vertical strips on the facades of Corpo A2 (Boeri Studio), recall the architectural style used in the other master plan buildings to convey a sense of unity to the complex.

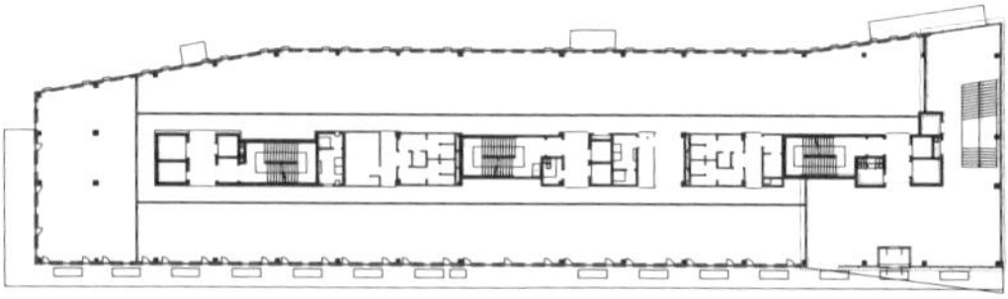

© Boeri Studio

© Paolo Rosselli

architects
Boeri Studio,
Barreca & La Varra

type
offices

construction
2001-2011

58. Church of the Resurrection of Jesus

Via Pisa 37
20099 Sesto San Giovanni

open to public

M1
Sesto 1° Maggio FS

700/702
Via Grandi - Via Pisa

Created according to the winning design in a competition launched by the CEI in 2004, and built in the industrial outskirts of Milan, this project was designed to replace a hangar-church built by worker-priests in the 1960s.
Through the fragmented lines of one side, the rectangular central body of the church forms a concave facade that envelopes the parvis area; the church is surrounded by elements of transition connected with the city like the parish hall and the sports field, accessible through a lower transversal buffer zone. The interior of the church, with two suspended lateral ceiling "sails", is lit by a series of skylights set between the roof beams, and a large opening in the end wall above the presbytery.
The entire church from the facade to the bell tower is clad in an abstract geometrical pattern of alternating sheets of sandstone and Trani stone.

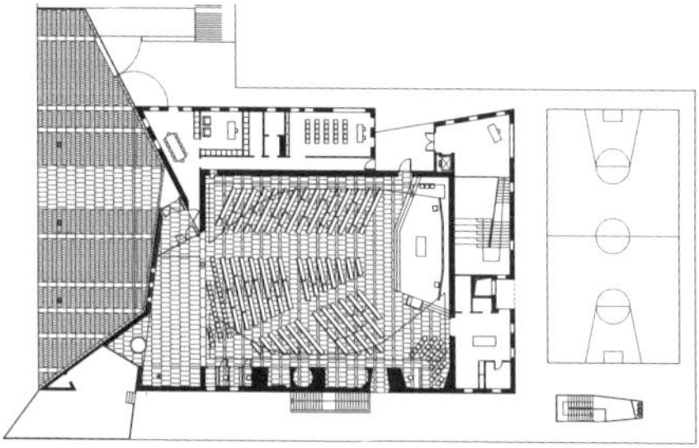

architects
Cino Zucchi Architetti

type
church

construction
2008-2010

59. New Campari Central Headquarters

Viale Antonio Gramsci 161
20099 Sesto San Giovanni

open to public

M1
Sesto 1° Maggio FS

701
Viale Gramsci -
Via Adua

Built on the location of the plant founded in 1904 by Davide Campari, the new Campari headquarters has maintained part of the original building enclosing it within the structure as a well-preserved example of Italian industrial archaeology.
The main complex is composed of two buildings. The first is a tower that houses the group headquarters' offices spread over nine floors above ground and two underground. The other building is bridged, and connected to the first structure at two underground floor levels, and at two above ground at the height of the fourth and fifth floors of the first structure. In addition is the original wing and the foyer, an open piazza covered with a curved laminated wooden roof covered externally with a planted green layer that slopes down to a shallow reflecting pool.
While the layout is a clever play on volumetric subtraction, the choice of materials is expressed through the combination of elements in steel, reinforced concrete and glued laminated wood. The green spaces and red brick cladding, homage to the company's traditions, bring strong colour impact making the Campari complex a landmark that stands out against the surrounding buildings.

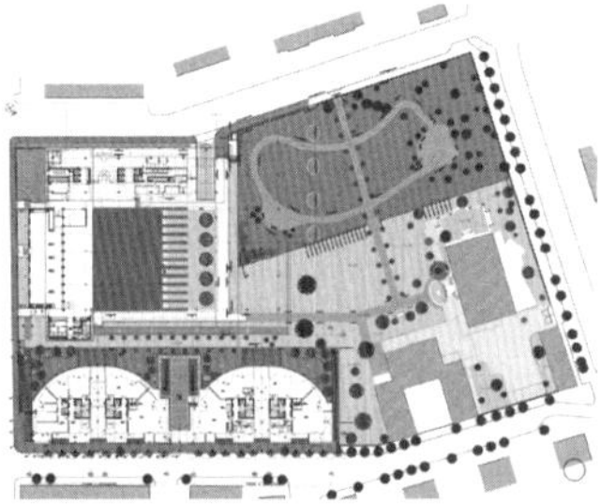

architects
Mario Botta,
Giancarlo Marzorati

type
residential, offices

construction
2006-2009

60. Redevelopment of the Bicocca Area and the Teatro degli Arcimboldi

Viale dell'Innovazione 20
20126 Milan

open to public

www.teatroarcimboldi.it

M5
Bicocca

87
Teatro degli Arcimboldi

The master plan project, which was the winning design in an international contest by invitation in 1985, concerns the redevelopment of the former Pirelli industrial zone, which covered an area of about 700,000 square metres and represented one of the largest and most complex decommissioned areas in Europe.
Based on a regular grid plan, the project faced the dual objective of maximum integration within the urban fabric of the city, and of defining a layout suitable for a range of diversified activities: a university campus, a research centre, and a residential area.
Among the most recent constructions is the Pirelli RE headquarters, that envelops the previous cooling tower, composed of a cube measuring 50 metres on each side, with three wings for office space, and a glazed facade overlooking the Bicocca degli Arcimboldi Park.
Offset on the grid is the Teatro degli Arcimboldi, initially built to replace the Teatro alla Scala during the theatre's restoration, with a fan-shaped auditorium (2,400 seating capacity) composed of a stalls area on two levels and two balconies, a fly tower 33 metres high, and a proscenium dimensioned to share stage sets with la Scala, plus two entrance foyers for access to the balconies.

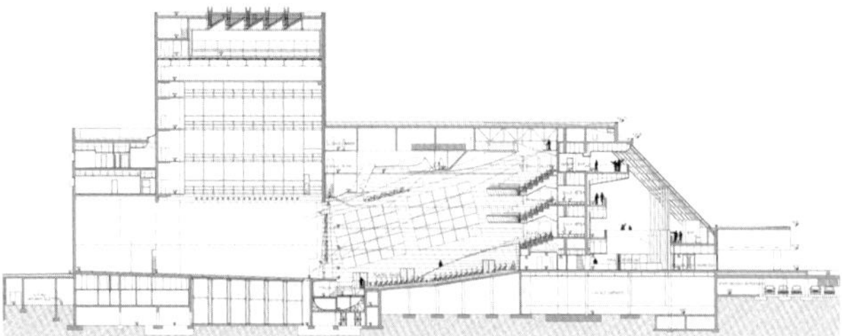

architects
Gregotti Associati

type
masterplan

construction
1994-2005

61. Deutsche Bank

Piazza del Calendario 3
20126 Milan

external viewing only

M5
Bicocca

S7/S8/S9/S11
Greco Pirelli

87
Viale dell'Innovazione - Via Figini

The original project for this urban block envisaged the construction of eight towers with a piazza in the centre, plus a sequence of porticos to provide access in two directions; however, Deutsche Bank requested a 33,000 square metre construction (equivalent of five towers) with a height limit of 32.40 metres, and, in agreement with the project, a ground floor portico.
Valle's project consists of a linear "Lombardy courtyard" style building, open towards the north and west, but closed on the southern side where it acts as an enclosing element of the Bicocca area, and no longer a portal open towards Milan. The Y-shaped form of the southern side and the offset position provided extra length and also determined the new orientation of the piazza facing the Collina dei Ciliegi (Cherry tree hill). It also permitted the projection of the upper floors on the western block and a change in the side entrances that were narrowed and then disappeared completely from the south side.
A further urban element is the external cladding composed of glossy black marble on the base buildings and grey Repen marble on the upper floors: the reflective surface of the glossy black finish annuls the solidity of the base, and variations in light reflect the changes in weather in the pale grey surface of the upper floors.

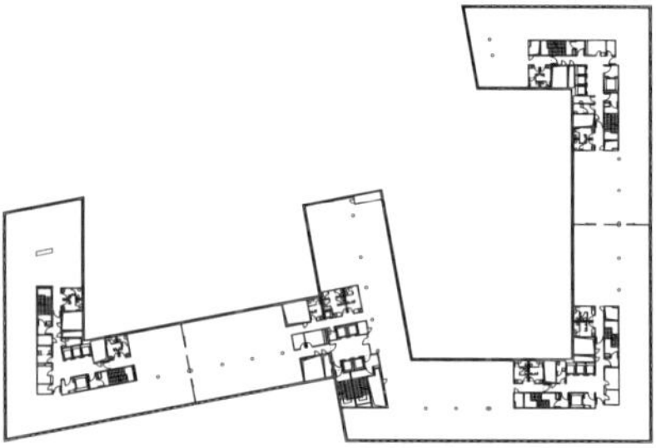

© Studio Valle Architetti Associati

architects
Studio Valle Architetti Associati

type
offices

construction
1997-2005

62. Residential Home in the Villaggio dei Giornalisti

Via Ettore Perrone di San Martino 8
20125 Milan

external viewing only

42
Piazzale Farina

A model of rationalist architecture, the single-family house by Luigi Figini is located in the outskirts to the north east of the city in a zone which has now become a strongly built-up area, but which was previously surrounded by farmland and a green rural landscape.
The building is composed of a golden rectangle measuring 18x5.50 metres; the constant module maintains the vertical and horizontal proportions. It was constructed with a concrete bearing structure and cantilevered perimetral walls, and is positioned according to a heliothermic axis to create the best possible window/floor surface ratio. Raised above ground level set on equidistant stilt columns, the first level is composed of a kitchen, a second bedroom, and a living room open onto a double height terrace. On the second floor is the private area with the main bedroom and bathroom, and two terraces, one equipped as a workout gym, and the other with a small pool set in the flooring.
The facades are clad in a white plaster finish and the long strip windows of the first floor are echoed in the upper level walls where the structural beams suspended around the perimeter of the building, are left visible.

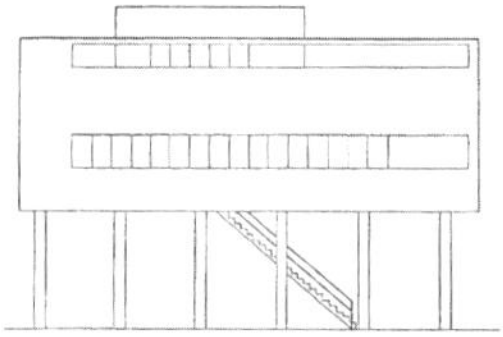

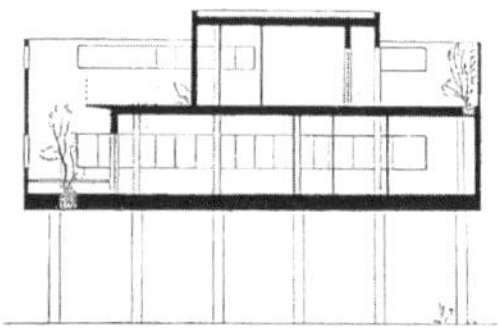

architects
Luigi Figini

type
residential

construction
1933-1935

63. MAC 5-6-7

Via Carlo Imbonati 18
20159 Milan

external viewing only

M3
Maciachini

70
Via Imbonati -
Via Monte San Genesio

Positioned on top of an artificial plateau, 1,3 metres above street level, this complex is composed of three buildings; the first is set parallel to Via Imbonati, creating continuity with the existing building facades, and the other two are connected by a glazed atrium, arranged to form an H-shape, with one end occupying the right-angled corner between Via Imbonati and Via Bracco. The buildings are designed so that every floor can be subdivided into several rental units.
The interiors can be laid out either as open-plan spaces or partitioned into sequences of single or double cellular offices. In all configurations, meeting rooms can either be located in the internal space, or can occupy the corner locations of each floor, enjoying triple aspect views as well as natural ventilation and light.
As in other previous projects, here too Sauerbruch and Hutton opted for experimental colour treatment on the vertical surfaces conceived as a mosaic composed of sheets of glass, screen-printed on the rear side, and with differentiated colour groups and scale on the various facades chosen according to their urban context (ochre, red and pink on the boundary facades, green and blue facing the walkway, and neutral colours on the façades next to the atrium).

© Sauerbruch Hutton

architects
Sauerbruch Hutton

type
offices

construction
2008-2010

64. MAC 9 - Zurich Headquarters

Via Benigno Crespi 23
20159 Milan

external viewing only

4
Valassina

M3
Maciachini

70
Via Imbonati -
Via Monte San Genesio

MAC 9, the headquarters of the Zurich Insurance Company, is part of the master plan project for the redevelopment of the former Carlo Erba industrial area, based on opening up the zone towards the city centre while maintaining the local urban fabric and direct access to the adjacent park.
The complex is composed of a two-storey base that acts as a link between the different heights. It supports the tall C-shaped building that encloses a large internal open space containing a garden planted with tall mature trees.
The first floor supported by a huge row of V-shaped pillars overlooks a raised piazza facing the garden, and forms the distribution area for the offices, acting as the core area for the common activities of the company; on the upper floor of the base block is an auditorium composed of an irregular truncated pyramid volume, while on the top floor is a glass and iron geodesic structure created in the top south-west corner of the building: its rounded profile represents a panoramic lantern shining towards the city centre.

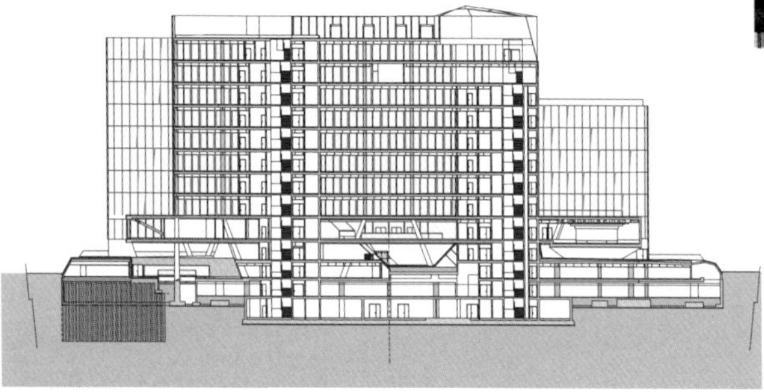

architects
Alessandro Scandurra –
Scandurra Studio
Architettura

type
offices

construction
2006-2011

65. "Living in Milan" project – Via Senigallia

Via Senigallia
20161 Milan

external viewing only

M3
Comasina

41
Via Senigallia -
Via Oroboni

This project began in a context to incorporate wider urban aspects, not limited to an area enclosed between the Milano-Venezia motorway and the Milano-Meda highways, developed in an irregular and fragmented manner over time. The solution proposed by the project was to seek a new identity for the area through the recovery of large open spaces. The hybrid configuration of this complex includes internal spaces, that are protected but fluid at the same time, with small piazzas and green spaces where the local population is encouraged to meet and spend leisure time, as well as tree-planted external areas that connect the area to the urban centre. The four main buildings establish a clear perimeter forming a composition surrounding a rhomboid-shaped centre courtyard area that hosts buildings for the community: three pavilions for cultural and leisure activities, a work-out gym, stores and restaurants, office space, a multi-service health centre, and a system of gardening allotments. The striking facades create impact with their dominating styles. On one building the smooth rose and brown surfaces are interrupted by vertical slots containing panels and window openings; in the other building the bathroom and kitchen areas in solid blocks contrast with the voids of the balcony terraces alongside, creating a regular chess-board effect.

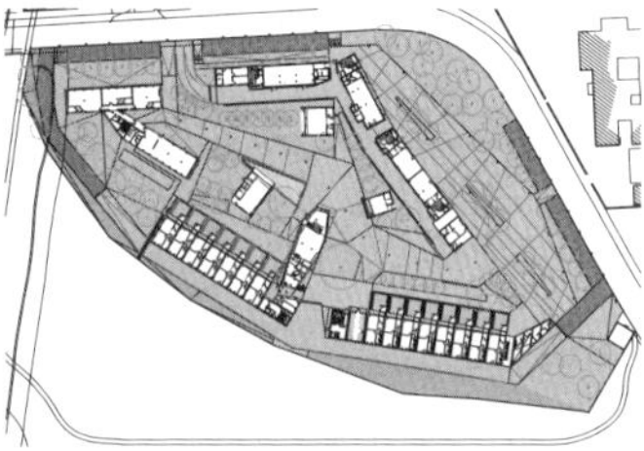

architects
Remo Dorigati_OdA Associati

type
residential

construction
2005-2012

66. Bi - La Fabbrica del Gioco e delle Arti

Via Gianni Rodari 3
20032 Cormano

open to public

www.bilafabbrica
delgiocoedellearti.it

S4
Cusano Milanino

This prize-winning project of the architectural contest in 2004 deals with the renovation of the cotton mill in the small industrial town of Cormano, transformed in 1999 in a new residential neighbourhood.
The intervention consisted of a redevelopment scheme aimed at repurposing the building; the demolition work was limited to only the strictly necessary, conserving walls and flooring, with the insertion of new exhibition spaces and areas for learning activities. Since the existing spaces were not very flexible because of the limited changes made to the original building, additional volume was added to the main structure to house a flexible theatrical space that could be used for multiple purposes.
From this viewpoint, the building was conceived like a huge chest of drawers from which further elements can be pulled out like containers for games and toys. The building features several playful elements such as the zebra-striped facade and the arrangement of irregular columns not connected for any structural reasons.

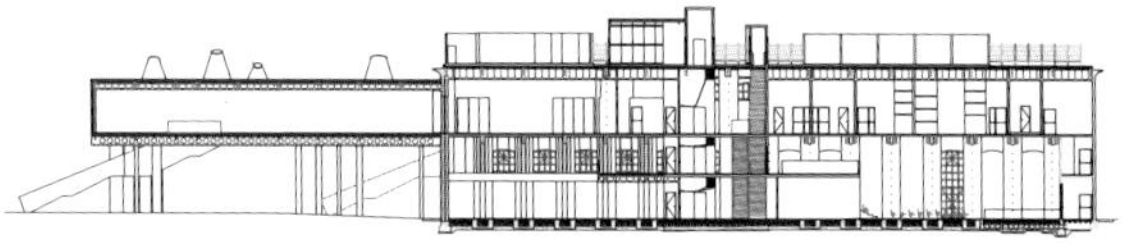

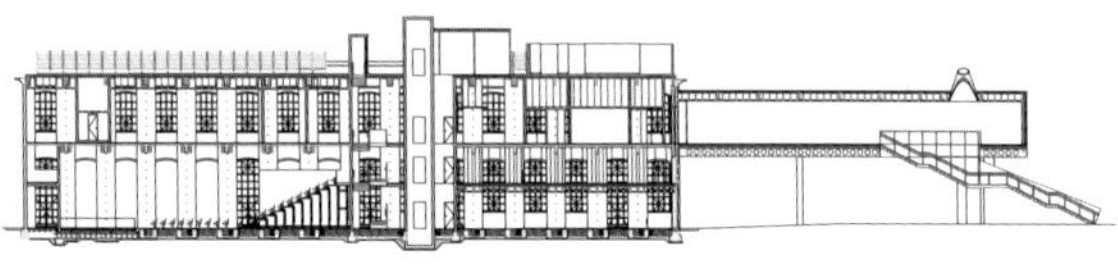

architects
5+1AA

type
library, studios, exhibition, theatre

construction
2005-2010

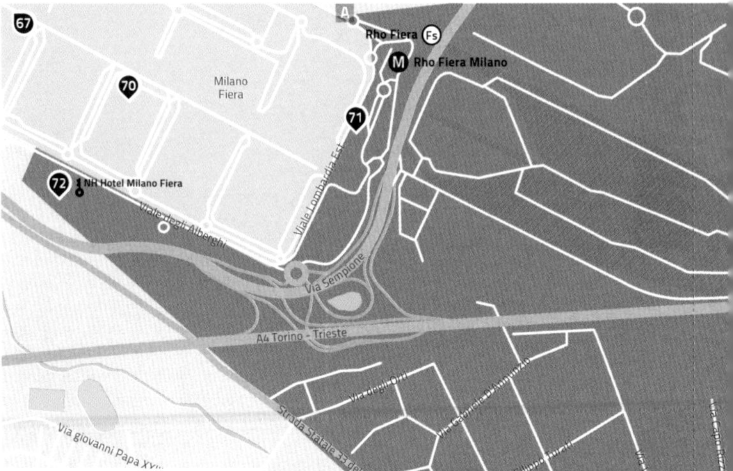
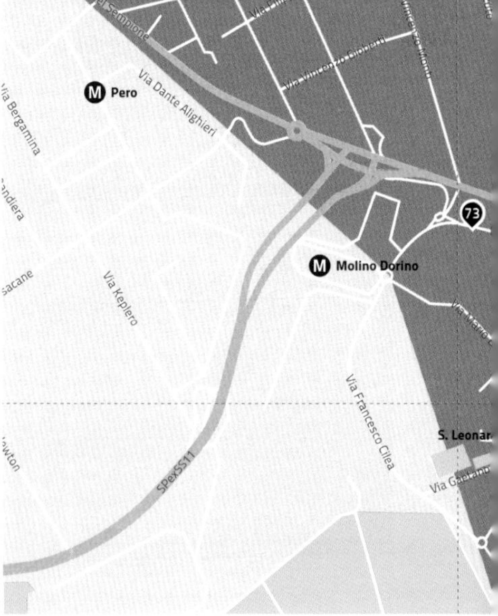

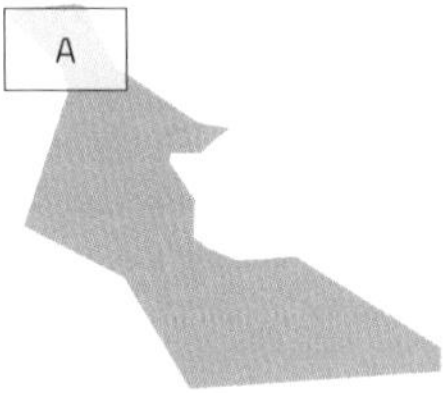

Greater Milan

67. Perfetti Van Melle Factory
68. Expo Master plan 2015
69. Italian Pavilion Milan Expo 2015
70. New Milan Trade Fair
71. Horizontal Office Block Tower
72. NH Hotel Fiera
73. "Living in Milan" project – Via Gallarate
74. "Monte Amiata" Apartment Complex
75. Social Housing at Portello

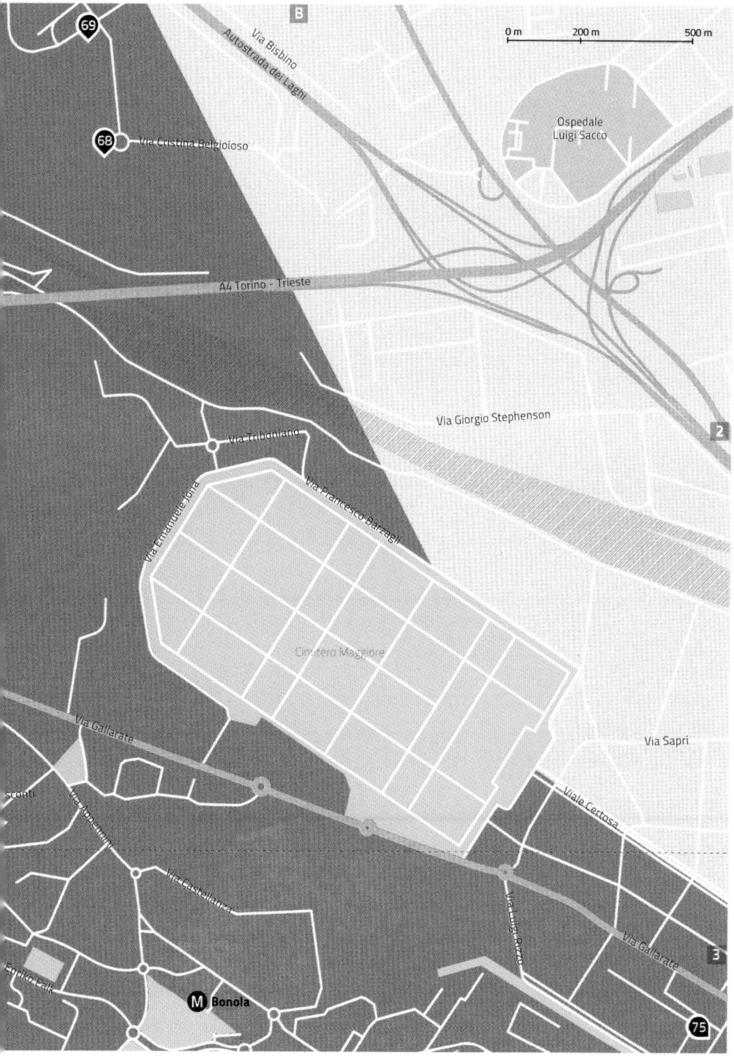

B
0 m
200 m
500 m
69
68
Via Cristina Belgioioso
Via Bisbino
Autostrada dei Laghi
Ospedale
Luigi Sacco
A4 Torino - Trieste
Via Giorgio Stephenson
2
Via Triboniano
Via Emanuele Jona
Via Francesco Barzagli
Cimitero Maggiore
Via Gallarate
Via Sapri
sconti
Via Appennini
Viale Certosa
Via Castellanza
Via Luigi Rizzo
Via Gallarate
3
Enriko Falk
Bonola
75

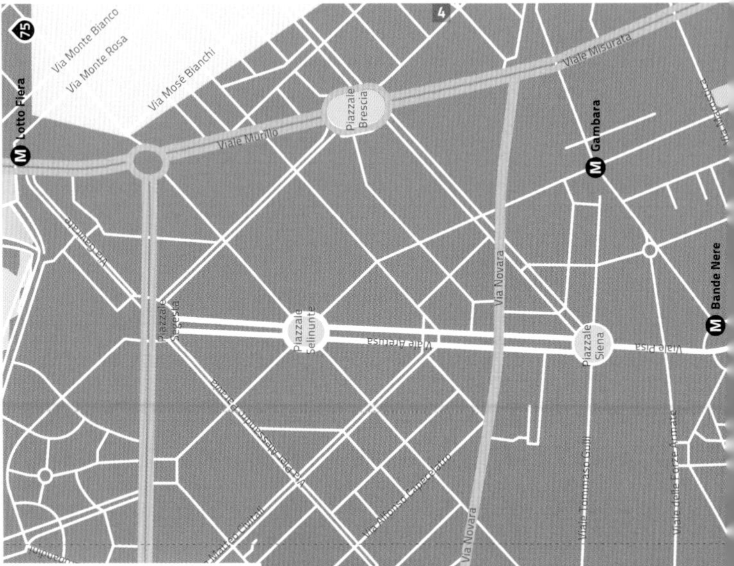

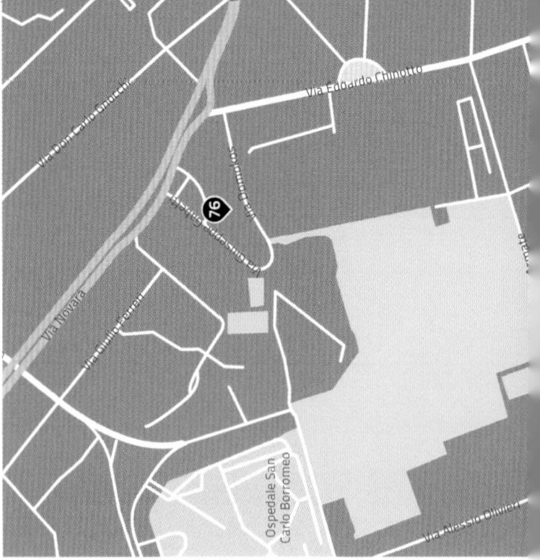

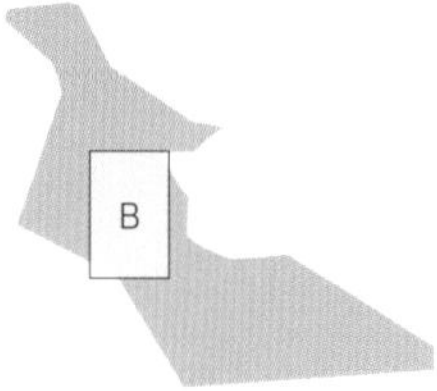

Greater Milan

75. Social Housing at Portello
76. Social Housing in Via Cenni
77. Istituto Marchiondi Spagliardi
78. Bertieri 4
79. Piazza Tirana Apartment Tower

5
0 m
200 m
500 m
C
B
78
Via Ettore Romagnoli
Via Giacinto Bruzzesi
Via Gentile Bellini
Piazza Pietro Frattini
Via Lorenteggio
Via Bartolomeo D'Alviano
Viale S. Gimignano
Via Luigi Soderini
Via Arzaga
Via Francesco Primaticcio
Primaticcio
Il luogo di Aimo e Nadia
Via Cascina Corba
Via delle Mimose
Giardino Alberto Moravia
Via Angelo Inganni
Inganni
Via della Rondine
Via Giambellino
Milano S. Cristoforo
Piazza Tirana
79
Via Pietro Giordani
Via Bisceglie
Via Zurigo
Bisceglie
Via Creta
77

67. Perfetti Van Melle Factory

Via XXV Aprile 7
20020 Lainate

external viewing only

Z617
Via Re Umberto I -
Via Lamarmora

The project was aimed at renovating an existing industrial plant located in an area on the outskirts of Milan, with open landscapes and recent residential expansion. The intervention involved building a new office building, warehouse space and a loading bay area. The project also focussed on the reorganisation and new design of the parking areas, internal green-planted spaces and handling areas.
The various new constructions are linked by a single semi-transparent urban wall, 200 metres long and 16 metres high that also encloses the green space called the "Birch garden". A metal curtain was created using about 200 frames made from L-shaped galvanised profiles assembled to form a continuous grid system. The structure was filled with perforated plate panels on which forty thousand glass disks were applied. The disks are in two sizes and three different finishes: transparent, glossy satin and opaque satin finishes. The natural daylight and in particular, the nocturnal lighting system installed at the base of the facade, changes the colours of the disks providing strong scenographic impact along the wall surface facing the city, becoming a new symbol for the company and for its products.

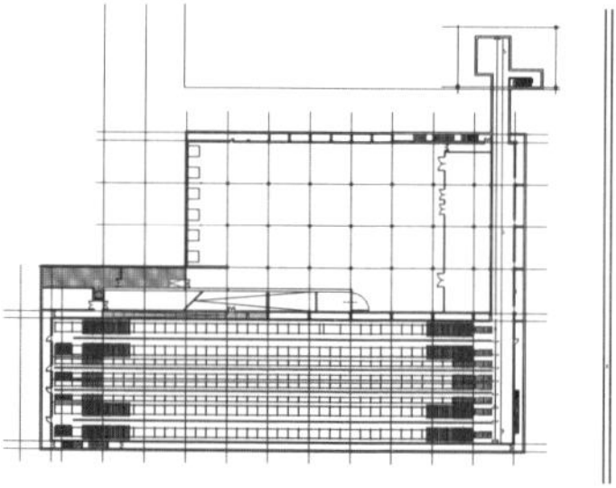

© Archea Associati

architects
Archea Associati

type
offices, warehouse

construction
2005-2011

68. Expo Master plan 2015

Area Expo 2015
20145 Rho

open to public

www.expo2015.org

M1
Rho Fiera

The Master plan for Expo 2015, that is focussed on the concept "Feeding the Planet, Energy for Life" , is the result of a series of processes that began with a concept plan drawn up by an international team of consulting architects in 2009.
The layout of the area, inspired by the structure of the castrum, the structural core of ancient Roman cities, is composed of the intersection of two perpendicular avenues: the Cardo (350 metres) that runs from north to south and houses the Italian exhibition spaces, and the Decumano (1,500 metres) running in an east-west direction, lined with the (self-built) pavilions of the participating countries, plus the clusters or exhibition spaces that bring together countries that produce or have a relationship with a specific food.
At the four ends of the main axes are the Collina Mediterranea, (Mediterranean Hill), the Expo Centre, the Open Air Theatre and the Lake Arena, the main orientation points, but also the focal points for the most important events of the exposition. The perimeter of the site will have a series of bioclimatic greenhouses that reproduce most of the planet's ecosystems; it is entirely surrounded by water to recall the landscape of the Milan canal system.

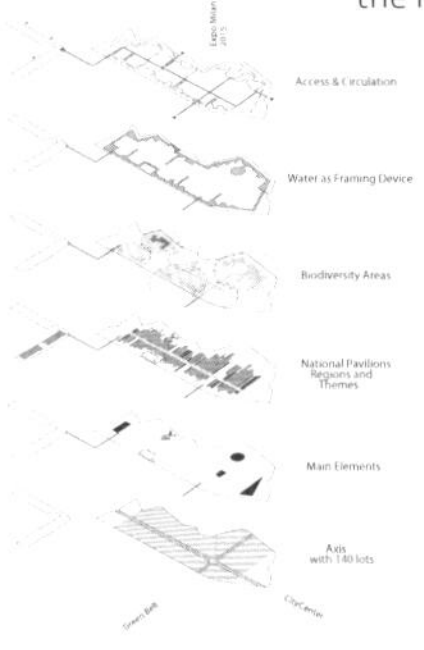

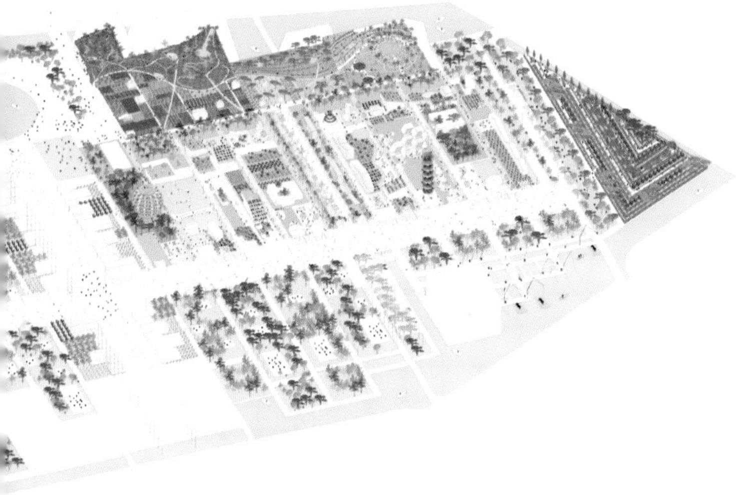

architects
Stefano Boeri, Richard Burdett, Jacques Herzog, William McDonough and Joan Busquets, Società Expo 2015

type
master plan

construction
2013-2015

69. Italian Pavilion Milan Expo 2015

Area Expo 2015
20145 Rho

open to public

www.padiglione
italiaexpo2015.com

M1
Rho Fiera

Based on the winning design in the international contest held in 2013, Palazzo Italia is built along the Cardo to create a scenographic backdrop; the project is composed of the main pavilion six storeys high, covering a surface of 13,700 square metres, and a series of three storey temporary buildings that cover 10,000 square metres.
Inspired by the "Urban forest", the outer shell of Palazzo Italia is composed of interwoven branches symbolising an idea of cohesion and community, and an internal piazza designed as a symbolic heart that forms the starting point for the exhibition circuit. It is surrounded by the four buildings of the Exhibition zone (West Block), the Auditorium-Events zone (South Block) the building for State and government representative offices (North Block) and the Meeting and Conference zone (East Block).
Based on sustainability principles, the construction has been achieved almost energy free thanks to the solar panel roof covering and the photocatalytic cement used on the external shell, whose active ingredients react with sunlight to capture atmospheric pollution and convert it to inert salts.

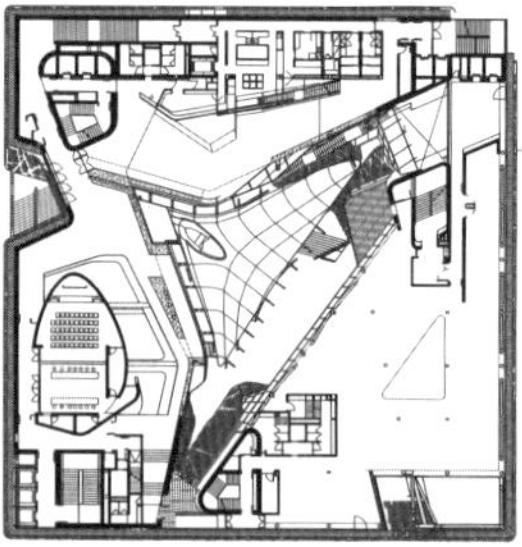

architects	type	construction
Nemesi&Partners	pavilion	2013-2015

70. New Milan Trade Fair

Strada Statale 33
del Sempione 28
20145 Rho

open to public

www.fieramilano.it

M1
Rho Fiera

S5/S6/S11/S14
Rho Fiera

The New Milan Trade Fair covering a surface of over 2 million square metres was built in the area of the former Rho-Pero Agip oil refineries based on the prize-winning project of the international contest by invitation.
The layout is composed of a central east-west axis 1,500 metres long, arranged in a straight line and developed on two levels: eight rectangular pavilions are arranged symmetrically on the northern and southern sides of the centre axis, including the Congress and Services Centre and a large range of cafés, restaurants, offices, hotels, shopping arcades and conference rooms. The iconic element is the roofing over the central walkway composed of a "sail" in a reticular steel and glass structure supported by branching columns. The sail is built of non-standard components which are not interchangeable and whose horizontal flow is moulded at the main junction points to create organic "craters", "waves", "dunes" and "hills". In the centre of the complex, over the Congress and Services Centre, the "sail" soars vertically upwards to a height of 37 metres creating a peak in the form of a volcano (called "Logo") partly screened by elements in aluminium.

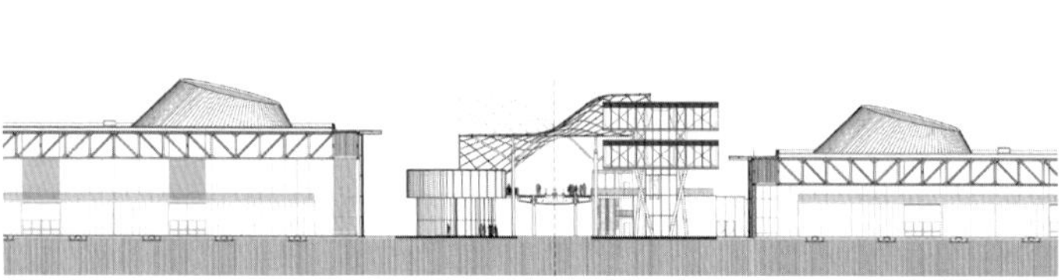

© Archivio Fuksas

architects
Massimiliano and Doriana Fuksas

type
exhibition hall

construction
2002-2005

71. Horizontal Office Block Tower

Largo Metropolitana 5
20017 Rho

external viewing only

M1
Rho Fiera

S5/S6/S11/S14
Rho Fiera

This office block houses the administration headquarters of the Fair Foundation and is part of the series of architectural projects built for the new Milan Trade Fair District by Massimilano Fuksas, Mario Bellini (multi-storey car park), Dominique Perrault (hotels) and LAND (public area landscaping).
The complex, composed of two adjacent thirteen-storey buildings connected by a full-height glazed foyer, is wrapped in a double skin: the internal layer in smoked grey glass, and the exterior covered with gold coloured brise-soleil slats, that define the facade with a play of light and reflection and opaque and transparent surfaces, gradually diminishing in number, protecting the north side of the building, while revealing the façade on the south side.
Further experimentation was applied on the black base level that separates pedestrian and vehicle access and includes a series of different service areas (office spaces, double height cafeteria, and foyer) at the top of which is a vertical garden with a sequence of slot openings that allow viewers to approach the transparent perimeter, and the horizontal, double-height transparent strip at fifth floor level.

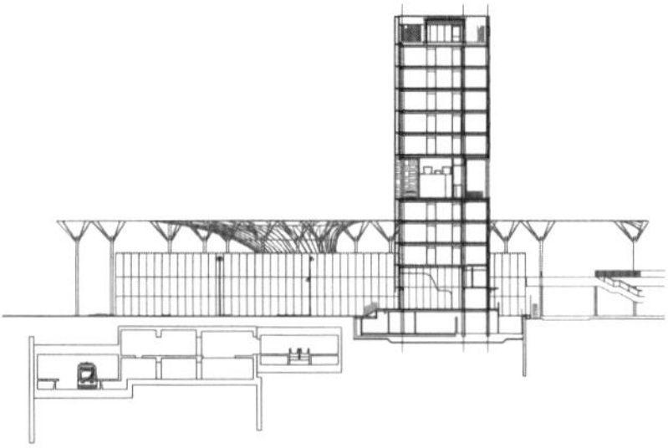

architects
5+1AA, Pietri Architects

type
offices, lecture hall

construction
2008-2010

72. NH Hotel Fiera

Viale degli Alberghi 17
20017 Rho

open to public

www.nh-hotels.it/
NH-Milano-Fiera

M1
Rho Fiera

S5/S6/S11/S14
Rho Fiera

528
Strada Statale
del Sempione -
Via Battisti

The French architect Dominique Perrault inserted the two towers of the NH Hotel Fiera into the grid layout of the Trade Fair District applying traditional urban architecture focusing on simple sobriety.
Two pure geometrical forms make up the design of the two towers: two parallelepipeds with a square base that rise for over sixty metres, almost seeming to lean away from one another because of their 5-degree angle. The taller, twenty-floor tower leans toward the Fair Ground in a northern direction, while the other eighteen-floor building towers over the pedestrian entrance. An irregular layout of over 1,000 windows contrasts with the 20,000 black bonded porcelain and glass tile facade. The configuration is the same for both towers and hotel rooms are arranged around the vertical façade perimeters, while a large central core contains the elevators, raising equipment, technical service rooms, and energy systems. A shining gold metal cruciform structure at the foot of the towers houses the hotel reception.

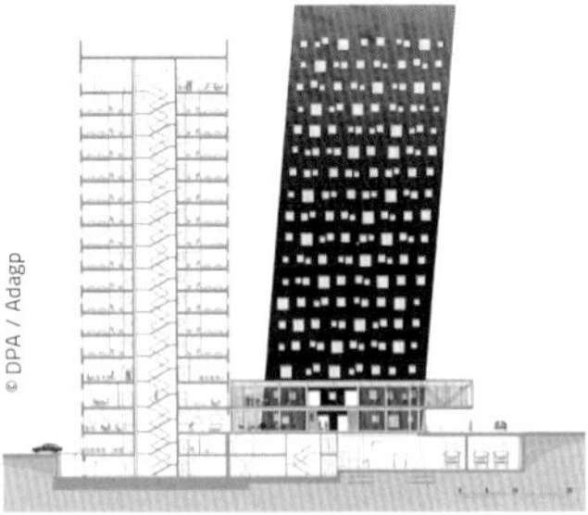

© DPA / Adagp

architects
Dominique Perrault architecture

type
hotel

construction
2007-2008

73. "Living in Milan" project – Via Gallarate

Via Gallarate, Via Appennini
20151 Milan

external viewing only

M1
Molino Dorino

72
Via Gallarate -
Via Appennini

This project proposes a social housing model where the residential complex is supported by a strong public space structure. The concept of "living" is therefore not limited to the personal space, but is extended to internal common areas, open public spaces, leisure areas, and services in the vicinity.
The complex is built along the margin between the urban fabric of Gallarate and the countryside around Milan, and aims at recreating the relationship between the buildings and green space with a park to serve the whole area. In this way, the ground level, which is, extremely rich in open public spaces, will become the true backbone of the project with a promenade path for pedestrians and cyclists, interspersed with small squares, sports and leisure areas, and services for the community.
The four residential buildings are constructed in a space between the high-rise complexes in Via Appennini, to guarantee the best possible exposition. The constructions include both horizontal blocks and towers: inside the park the three storey structures are integrated into the original walled sloping terrain, while to the southern end are four, eight, and ten-storey towers.

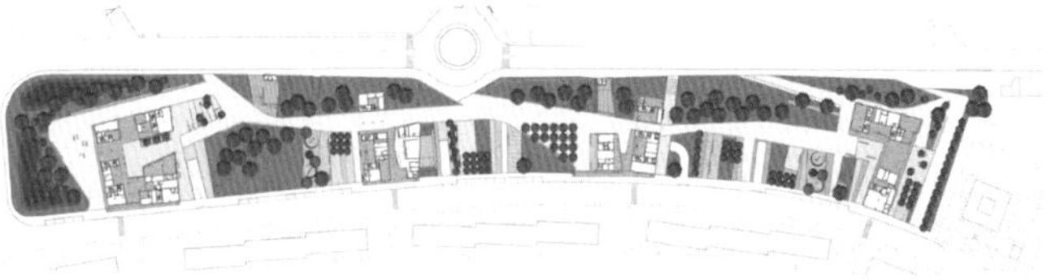

architects
MAB arquitectura –
Floriana Marotta,
Massimo Basile

type
residential

construction
2005-2009

74. "Monte Amiata" Apartment Complex

Via Francesco Cilea 106
20151 Milan

external viewing only

M1
San Leonardo

69
Via Cilea - Via Fichera

This complex constructed for the Monte Amiata Mining Company in a thirty-acre plot devoid of any historical or natural references, is composed of five long buildings of varying heights and sizes arranged in a fan-shaped layout.

The concept of social aggregation is expressed through the creation of a series of meeting spaces based on the concatenation of various galleries and balconies, horizontal and vertical paths, especially in the three piazzas, one of which houses an open-air theatre.

As part of the project, Carlo Aymonino assigned Aldo Rossi with the task of designing one of the residential apartment buildings. Based on the design of the traditional Lombardy balconied row houses, it is composed of a rectangular block raised on a row of reinforced concrete septa interrupted by two pairs of pillars. The facades are punctuated by the regular repetition of square windows divided into four, which was to become a recurring pattern in Rossi's architectural design.

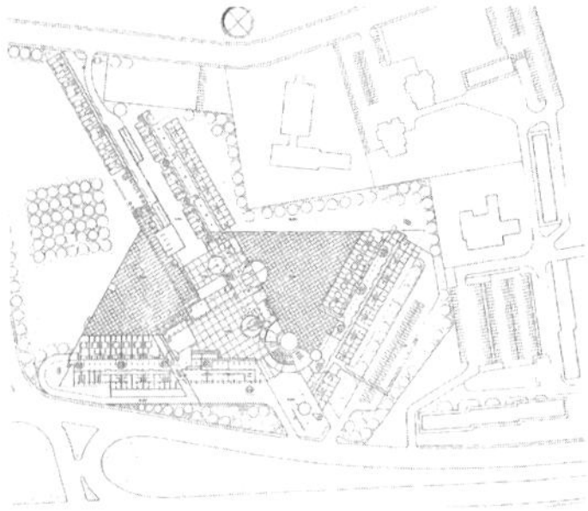

architects
Carlo Aymonino,
Aldo Rossi

type
residential

construction
1967-1974

75. Social Housing at Portello

Via Marco Ulpio Traiano
20149 Milan

external viewing only

M1
QT8

48
Viale Certosa - Via Grosotto

As part of the vast master plan for the redevelopment of the wider area conceived by Gino Valle, this complex is integrated in an urban fabric that combines late 19th century architecture and the experimental QT8 "green-city" plan.
This complex recalls examples of the composition and constructive styles of Milanese residential architecture in the fifties and sixties and consists of a series of interventions of different types: three residential buildings in the southern area at right angles to Viale Serra and based on the courtyard layout, two subsidised apartment towers facing largo Zanuso, clad with bleached terracotta tiles and white stone, with different types of window and hinged and roll down shutters, and the three free market apartment towers facing the communal gardens, clad in stone of various sizes and colours, with personal attached balconies arranged in an irregular manner.
Facing Via Traiano is the building that houses the IPER showroom and offices. It is clad in Cardoso stone and maintains the footprint and height of the former Alfa Romeo plant cafeteria. The building's facade on Via Traiano has also been maintained and now forms the new entrance to the building.

© Cino Zucchi Architetti

architects	type	construction
Cino Zucchi Architetti	residential	2002-2008

76. Social Housing in Via Cenni

Via Quinto Cenni
20147 Milan

external viewing only

64/72/80
Piazza Amati -
Via Novara

Constructed according to the prize-winning project of the competition held in 2009, this project represents an experiment in sustainability and high-rise eco-wooden construction.
The complex houses 123 apartments, mainly aimed at a market for singles or young families with controlled rents or future purchase agreement, and is composed of a two storey construction with a covered walkway access on the first floor, four 9-storey towers (among the tallest in Europe using this construction technology) and a range of common use areas such as hanging gardens and football field.
The construction technique consisting of cross-laminated timber panels, (X-lam), is used for the attic spaces as well as the internal and external walls. This construction features insulating panels and the use of natural biocompatible materials, and together with its focus on high environmental sustainability, it applies innovative technological systems such as radiant floor heating panels supplied from a system that uses the geothermal source of groundwater through heat pumps, and a mechanical ventilation system to improve air quality.

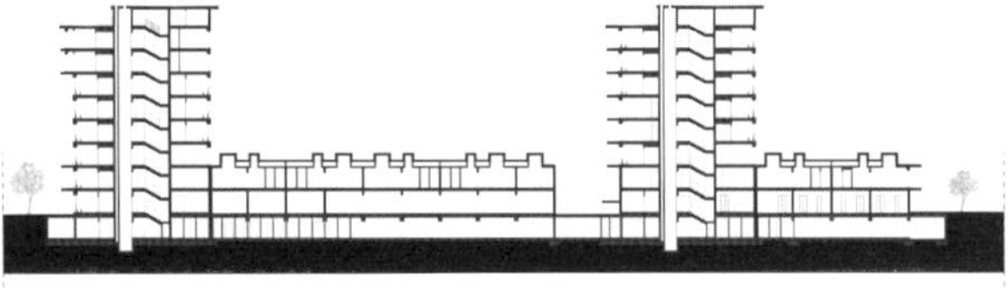

architects
ROSSIPRODI ASSOCIATI

type
residential

construction
2011-2013

77. Istituto Marchiondi Spagliardi

Via Noale 1
20152 Milan

external viewing only

58
Via Mosca - Via Noale

Following the destruction of the original building in Via Quadronno, during the bombing in World War II, a competition by invitation was launched for a new design for the Istituto Marchiondi Spagliardi, which was to house three hundred "problem boys" between the ages of 6 and 11, housing them in a boarding school and providing them with an education.
This complex, described by Reyner Banham as the symbol of neobrutalism in Italy, is composed of four structures: the office and management spaces, the student boarding school, the teachers' wing, and the school area. The project featured the use of exposed concrete and bright colours on the window and doorframes, floors and walls. From a social viewpoint, it was proposed as an experiment as a new educational model, based on the elimination of walls and bars, replacing the dormitories with duplex units and personal bathrooms, and the creation of spaces that encouraged socialising and meeting together.
Despite certain proposals to redevelop the building, some even quite recent, today the structure is in a state of deterioration following a periods of abusive occupation and several evacuations.

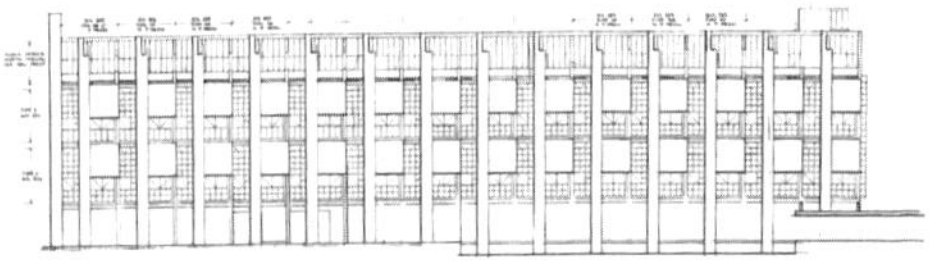

architects
Vittoriano Viganò

type
socio-educational institute

construction
1953-1957

78. Bertieri 4

Via Raffaello Bertieri 4
20146 Milan

external viewing only

50/61
Via Lorenteggio -
Via Tolstoj

Located in an area typical of the irregular urban expansion that evolved in the sixties and seventies, this building is part of a block dedicated to service industries in a zone characterised by irregular and interrupted facades along the street.
The project involved the redevelopment of an existing construction where the main structure was maintained while the façade, layout and spatial volume were modified with the construction of a new roof level. The heart of the building is a narrow rectangular inner courtyard, designed as a patio-garden to provide a pleasant view for the offices facing onto the inner space that also includes a new elliptic staircase adding further light.
The lower floor forms the entrances and foyers and the facades are clad in sandstone; three floors are dedicated to office space, closed by a curtain wall protected by external awnings, covered with new roofing composed of metal railings and horizontal projecting elements that act as a brise-soleil.

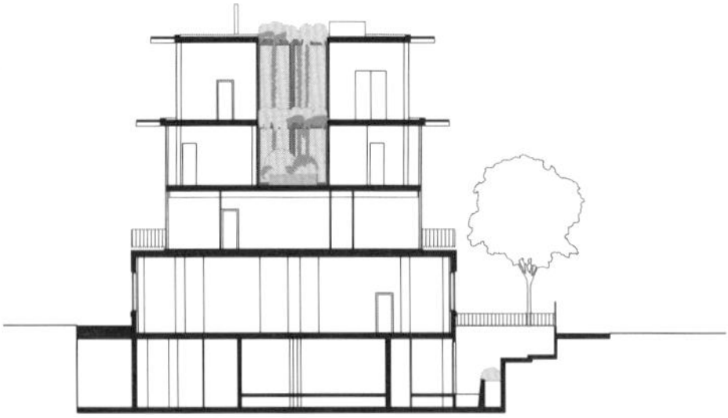

© Arassociati

© Vittorio Dozio

architects
Arassociati

type
offices

construction
2008-2009

79. Piazza Tirana Apartment Tower

Piazza Tirana 25
20147 Milan

external viewing only

S9
San Cristoforo

49
Piazza Tirana -
San Cristoforo

This project dealt with the subject of recovering an area on the outskirts of the city which featured a fragmented mixture of different building types (tall and low buildings, small industrial plants, residential housing, all without any strategic urban planning). The area is close to the main Milano-Vigevano highway, and is the site for certain important infrastructures such as the Naviglio Grande and the Milano-Mortara railway line. The vertical effect was sought through the proportions of the volumes as well as the inclusion of a slot, 2.5 metres wide, running the whole height of the building, creating a transparent column of light and giving a through view of the Naviglio and the railway lines. The facades are clad with concrete slab (GRC) blended with pigments, resins, glass fibre and iron filings to recall the colour of rolling stock.
The complex proposes apartments of various sizes, a condominium workout gym in the glazed section on the roof, and a winter garden on the ninth and tenth floors filtered by horizontal concrete brise-soleil slats.

architects
Quattroassociati

type
residential

construction
2003-2006

80. Milanofiori Nord Apartment Building

Via Roggia Bartolomea
20090 Assago

external viewing only

M2
Assago Milanofiori

352
Assago Milanofiori M2

This building is part of a much larger urban project that includes office buildings, a hotel, restaurants, and a movie theatre in an area close to Assago, on the south side of Milan.
The building has a C-shaped footprint and encircles a public park area overlooked by 110 apartments, all designed with double aspect windows and views. The side facing the street is more enclosed, and features sliding openwork wooden panels that screen sunlight into the apartments, while the internal facade is composed of large glazed surfaces and deep terraces that overlook the common garden area to create a continuation between inside and outside space. The internal-external transition is increased by a "winter garden", zone between the apartment and the terrace that changes the living space according to the seasons. Bioclimatic control of the whole complex is guaranteed by the tiered design that provides maximum exposition to sun while maintaining the privacy of the inhabitants.
The project is designed to internalise the surrounding area, a densely populated urban landscape, by working to support the aims proposed by the project: the interconnection between the use of technology and the successful outcome of the intervention.

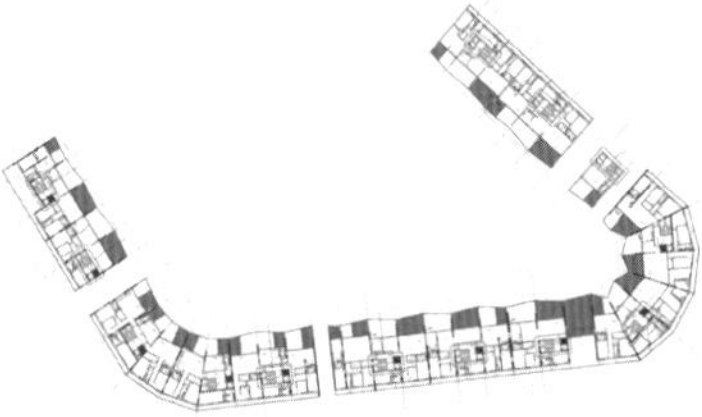

architects
OBR Open
Building Research

type
residential

construction
2005-2010

81. Nestlé Headquarters

Via del Mulino 6
20090 Assago

external viewing only

M2
Assago Milanofiori

352
Assago Milanofiori M2

This project was based on an analysis of the articulated access system to the Milanofiori area, the inclusion of pedestrian and cycling paths, and the integration with the master plan design.
The complex is based on an enclosed courtyard layout conceived like a "secret garden" for the exclusive use of the employees, but providing extensive views for those using the pedestrian and cycling paths.
While the footprint of the building is compact and rational, from the facade perspective, it is divided into several blocks forming a more fragmented composition. The structure is divided into different portions designed like "suspended boxes" of various sizes and set at different heights and at slightly different angles. The building entrance faces a semi-urban piazza, and forms the continuation of the pedestrian access from south-west connected to the Metropolitan underground station, while vehicular traffic is directed to the opposite side of the complex in an area screened by an embankment; the raised level is encased in the terrain to create a private internal space that contains the blocks with the main services, set at different levels.

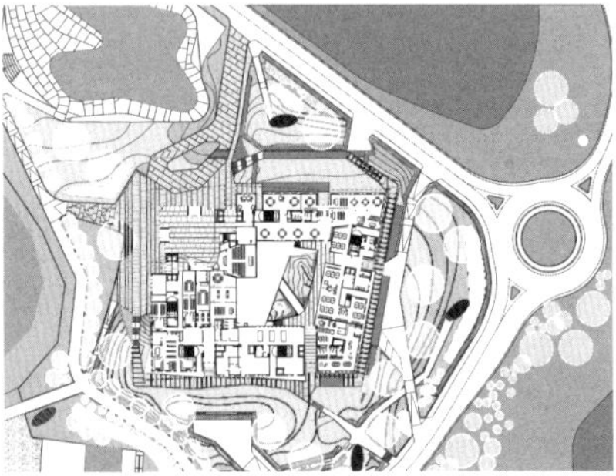

© Park Associati

architects
Park Associati

type
offices

construction
2012-2014

82. New BMW Headquarters

Via della Unione Europea 1
20097 San Donato Milanese

external viewing only

M3
San Donato Milanese

121
Via Emilia 20

Those who enter Milan from the Autosole motorway cannot help but notice the Headquarters of BMW Italia, set in the new Business District, the only part of the 1990 Tange masterplan that has been completed to date. The masterplan involves the development and expansion of San Donato Milanese, future satellite town with its "role of primary importance at international level as a suburb of Milan".
The initial impact might be the 42-metre, pure white tower silhouetted against the sky, or as it emerges from the fog, the fine black pattern of windowpanes and steel grid panels (coated with stucco Veneziano able to repel surface dust deposit). The complex is composed of three buildings whose layout echoes the company trademark, and that obey the requisites of seamless integration with the general plan for the area: one building is destined as a showroom, another as the Sales and Maintenance Centre, while the tower is dedicated to office space. The knife-blade side of the tower faces towards the motorway, from where it is perceived as a thin narrow building whose facade gently and gradually follows the curve of the road; the sharp wedge of the two top floors just below the crowning element juts out to stretch dynamically along the curve tangent.

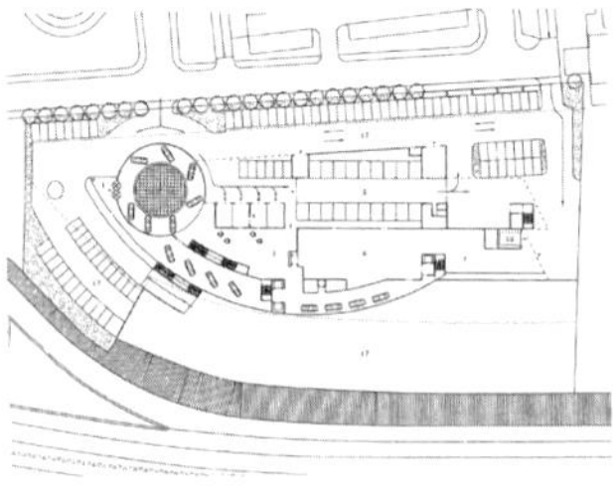

architects
Kenzo Tange

type
offices

construction
1995-1998

83. Fifth Building for ENI Office Complex

Via Konrad Adenauer, Via Mohandas K. Gandhi, Via Emilia
20097 San Donato Milanese

external viewing only

M3
San Donato Milanese

S1
San Donato Milanese

121
Via Emilia -
Viale De Gasperi

Prize-winning design in a competition by invitation in 1985, this complex is composed of a group of tiered buildings with rooftop hanging gardens that surround an internal park area including an artificial lake.
The facades are composed of coloured glass panels that permit a constant view of the internal green spaces, and are constructed of two separate walls with a 90 cm gap that provides considerable energy savings, improves environmental comfort and facilitates the development of the vertical greenhouse containing carefully selected plants. The building is surrounded by a grid construction of lacquered aluminium piping for both decorative and functional purposes to channel rain water.
Further towards the east is the third office building designed by Franco Albini, Franca Helg, Marco Albini and Antonio Piva (1969-1973): the four blocks are arranged in a cross formation around a distribution core. The building facade features distinctive horizontal bands and vertical cladding panels in red polyester plus an octagonal internal helical staircase.

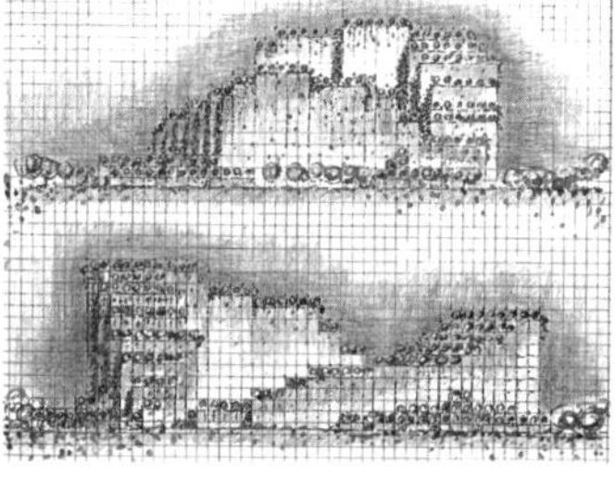

architects
Gabetti & Isola, Guido Drocco

type
offices

construction
1985-1992

Museums

Fondazione Prada
Temporary exhibitions
of contemporary art
-
Largo Isarco 2, 20139 Milan

www.fondazioneprada.org
info@fondazioneprada.org
Tel +39 02 56662611

Galleria d'Arte Moderna e
Padiglione d'Arte Contemporanea
Museum and temporary exhibitions of
contemporary art
-
Via Palestro 14-16, 20121 Milan

www.gam-milano.it; www.pacmilano.it
c.gam@comune.milano.it;
c.mostre@comune.milano.it
Tel +39 02 88445947; +39 02 88446359

Gallerie d'Italia
Museum of 19th and 20th
century art
-
Piazza della Scala 6, 20121 Milan

www.gallerieditalia.com
info@gallerieditalia.com
Tel +39 800 167619

Hangar Bicocca
Temporary exhibitions of
contemporary art
-
Via Chiese 2, 20126 Milan

www.hangarbicocca.org
info@hangarbicocca.org
Tel +39 02 66111573

Museo del Novecento
Museum of 20th century art
-
Via Guglielmo Marconi 1, 20122 Milan

www.museodelnovecento.org
museodelnovecento@civita.it
Tel +39 02 88444061

Museo Nazionale della Scienza e
della Tecnologia "Leonardo da Vinci"
Museum of Science and Technology
-
Via San Vittore 21, 20123 Milan

www.museoscienza.org
info@museoscienza.it
Tel +39 02 485551

Museo Poldi Pezzoli
Museum and temporary art exhibitions
-
Via Alessandro Manzoni 12, 20121
Milan

www.museopoldipezzoli.it
ferraris@museopoldipezzoli.it
Tel +39 02 794889

Palazzo Reale
Temporary art exhibitions
-
Piazza del Duomo 12, 20122 Milan

www.comune.milano.it/palazzoreale

Tel +39 02 0202

Pinacoteca di Brera
Art museum
-
Via Brera 28, 20121 Milan

www.brera.beniculturali.it
sbsae-mi.brera@beniculturali.it
Tel +39 02 72263264

Studio Museo Achille Castiglioni
Art Studio-museum
-
Piazza Castello 27, 20121 Milan

www.achillecastiglioni.it
info@achillecastiglioni.it
Tel +39 02 8053606

Triennale di Milano
Temporary exhibitions of architecture and design
-
Viale Emilio Alemagna 6, 20121 Milan

www.triennale.org
info@triennale.org
Tel +39 02 724341

Villa Necchi Campiglio
House-museum
-
Via Wolfango Amedeo Mozart 14, 20122 Milan

www.casemuseomilano.it
fainecchi@fondoambiente.it
Tel +39 02 76340121

Theatres

Auditorium di Milano
-
Largo Gustav Mahler, 20136 Milan

www.laverdi.org
info@auditoriumdimilano.org
Tel +39 02 83389401

Piccolo Teatro Strehler
-
Largo Antonio Greppi 1, 20121 Milan

www.piccoloteatro.org
info@piccoloteatro.org
Tel +39 02 42411889

Piccolo Teatro Studio Melato
-
Via Rivoli 6, 20121 Milan

www.piccoloteatro.org
info@piccoloteatro.org
Tel +39 02 42411889

Teatro alla Scala
-
Via Filodrammatici 2, 20121 Milan

www.teatroallascala.org
biglietteria@teatroallascala.org
Tel +39 02 88791

Teatro degli Arcimboldi
-
Viale dell'Innovazione 20, 20125 Milan

www.teatroarcimboldi.it
info@teatroarcimboldi.it
Tel +39 02 641142200

Teatro Franco Parenti
-
Via Pier Lombardo 14, 20135 Milan

www.teatrofrancoparenti.it
biglietteria@teatrofrancoparenti.it
Tel +39 02 59995206

Teatro Libero
-
Via Savona 1, 20144 Milan

www.teatrolibero.it
biglietteria@teatrolibero.it
Tel +39 02 8323126

Teatro Nazionale
-
Via Asti 2, 20149 Milan

www.teatronazionale.it
info@stage-entertainment.it
Tel +39 02 02 00640888

Restaurants

Al Fresco
•
Via Savona 50, 20144 Milan
www.alfrescomilano.it
info@alfrescomilano.it
Tel +39 02 4953 3630

Aromando Bistrot
•
Via Pietro Moscati 13, 20154 Milan
aromando@tiscali.it
Tel +39 02 36744172

Ceresio 7
• •
Via Ceresio 7, 20154 Milan
www.ceresio7.com
info@ceresio7.com
Tel +39 02 310 39221

Cracco
• • •
Via Victor Hugo 4, 20123 Milan
www.ristorantecracco.it
info@ristorantecracco.it
Tel +39 02 876774

d'O
• •
Via Magenta 18, San Pietro all'Olmo, 20010 Cornaredo
www.cucinapop.do
info@cucinapop.do
Tel +39 02 9362209

Dry
•
Via Solferino 33, 20121 Milan
www.drymilano.it
info@drymilano.it
Tel +39 02 63793414

Erba Brusca
•
Alzaia Naviglio Pavese 286, 20142 Milan
www.erbabrusca.it
info@erbabrusca.it
Tel +39 02 87380711

Il luogo di Aimo e Nadia
• • •
Via Privata Raimondo Montecuccoli 6, 20147 Milan
www.aimoenadia.com
info@aimoenadia.com
Tel +39 02 416886

La Brisa
• •
Via Brisa 15, 20123 Milan
www.ristorantelabrisa.it
info@ristorantelabrisa.it
Tel +39 02 86450521

Pont de Ferr
• •
Ripa di Porta Ticinese 55, 20143 Milan
www.pontdeferr.it
pontdeferr@gmail.com
Tel +39 02 89406277

Ratanà
• •
Via Gaetano de Castillia 28, 20124 Milan
www.ratana.it
info@ratana.it
Tel +39 02 87128855

Upcycle
•
Via Andrea Maria Ampère 59, 20131 Milan
www.upcyclecafe.it
info@upcyclecafe.com
Tel +39 02 83428268

Hotels

• • • expensive
• • mid-range
• inexpensive

Armani Hotel Milano
• • •
Via Alessandro Manzoni 31,
20121 Milan
milan.armanihotels.com/
milan@armanihotels.com
Tel +39 02 88838888

Enterprise Hotel
• •
Corso Sempione 91-93, 20149 Milan
www.enterprisehotel.com
info@enterprisehotel.com
Tel +39 02 318181

Grand Hotel et de Milan
• • •
Via Manzoni 29, 20121 Milan
www.grandhoteletdemilan.it
infos@grandhoteletdemilan.it
Tel +39 02 723141

Hotel Boscolo Milano
• • •
Corso Giacomo Matteotti 4-6,
20121 Milan
www.milano.boscolohotels.com
reservation@milano.boscolo.com
Tel +39 02 77679611

Hotel dei Cavalieri
• •
Piazza Giuseppe Missori 1,
20123 Milan
www.hoteldeicavalieri.com
booking@hoteldeicavalieri.com
Tel +39 02 88571

Hotel Excelsior Gallia
• • •
Piazza Duca d'Aosta 9, 20124 Milan
www.excelsiorhotelgallia.com
excelsior.hotelgallia@luxurycollection.com
Tel +39 02 67851

Hotel Palazzo Segreti
• •
Via San Tomaso 8, 20121 Milan
www.palazzosegreti.com
info@palazzosegreti.com
Tel +39 02 49529250

Hotel Straf
• • •
Via San Raffaele 3, 20121 Milan
www.straf.it
info@straf.it
Tel +39 02 805081

NH Hotel Fiera Milano
•
Viale degli Alberghi 17, 20017 Rho
www.nh-hotels.it/hotel/nh-milano-fiera
nhfiera@nh-hotels.com
Tel +39 02 300371

Nhow
• •
Via Tortona 35, 20144 Milan
www.nh-hotels.it/hotel/nhow-milano
info.nhow@nh-hotels.com
Tel +39 02 4898861

Nu Hotel
•
Via Feltre 19B, 20132 Milan
www.nu-hotel.com
info@nu-hotel.com
Tel +39 02 9715451

UNA Hotel Tocq
•
Via Alessio di Tocqueville 7D,
20154 Milan
www.unahoteltocq.com
una.tocq@unahotels.it
Tel +39 02 62071

Architectural offices

5+1AA
-
Via Giovanni Cadolini 32, 20137 Milan
www.5piu1aa.com
info@5piu1aa.com
Tel +39 02 54019701

Antonio Citterio
Patricia Viel and Partners
-
via Cerva 4, 20122 Milan
www.antoniocitterioandpartners.it
info@antoniocitterioandpartners.it
Tel +39 02 7638801

Arassociati
-
Via Correggio 18, 20149 Milan
www.arassociati.it
info@arassociati.it
Tel +39 02 72010046

Archea Associati
-
Piazzale Carlo Archinto, 9, 20159 Milan
www.archea.it
staffmilano@archea.it
Tel +39 02 69431300

Architetto Michele De Lucchi
-
Via Varese 15, 20121 Milan
www.amdl.it
amdl@amdl.it
Tel +39 02 6378681

Barreca & La Varra
-
Via Tito Vignoli 9, 20146 Milan
www.barrecaelavarra.it
info@barrecaelavarra.com
Tel +39 02 48029050

Cino Zucchi Architetti
-
Via Giuseppe Revere 8, 20123 Milan
www.zucchiarchitetti.com
studio@zucchiarchitetti.com
Tel +39 02 48016130

Consalez Rossi Architetti Associati
-
Via Giovanni Cadolini 32, 20137 Milan
www.consalezrossi.com
info@consalezrossi.com
Tel +39 02 36556312

David Chipperfield Architects
-
Via Vigevano 8, 20144 Milan
www.davidchipperfield.co.uk
info@davidchipperfield.it
Tel +39 02 83439150

Gregotti Associati International
-
Via Matteo Bandello 20, 20123 Milan
www.gregottiassociati.it
gai.milano@gregottiassociati-link.it
Tel +39 02 4814141

LAND Milano
-
Via Varese 16, 20121 Milan
www.landsrl.com
mail@landsrl.com
Tel +39 02 8069111

MAB Arquitectura –
Floriana Marotta, Massimo Basile
-
Via Tranquillo Cremona 27,
20145 Milan
www.mabarquitectura.com
info@mabarquitectura.com
Tel +39 02 5819991

Park Associati
-
Via Benvenuto Garofalo 31,
20133 Milan

www.parkassociati.com
info@parkassociati.com
Tel +39 02 798452

Piuarch
-
Via Palermo 1, 20121 Milan

www.piuarch.it
studio@piuarch.it
Tel +39 02 89096130

Quattroassociati
-
Piazza Sant'Ambrogio 25, 20123 Milan

www.quattroassociati.it
studio@quattroassociati.it
Tel +39 02 4981780

Scandurra Studio Architettura
-
Via Legnano 28, 20121 Milan

www.scandurrastudio.com
studio@scandurrastudio.com
Tel +39 02 29002261

Stefano Boeri Architetti
-
Via Gaetano Donizetti 4, 201122 Milan

www.stefanoboeriarchitetti.net
studio@stefanoboeriarchitetti.net
Tel +39 02 55014101

Studio Albori
-
Via Francesco Soave 24, 20135 Milan

www.albori.it
studio@albori.it
Tel +39 02 55180167

Studio Italo Rota & Partners
-
Via Fratelli Bronzetti 20, 20129 Milan

www.studioitalorota.it
info@studioitalorota.it
Tel +39 02 76115332

Studio Libeskind
-
Via Spadari 7-9, 20123 Milan

www.libeskind.com
info@libeskind.com
Tel +39 02 84502385

Studio Valle Architetti Associati
-
Via Aurelio Saffi 10, 20123 Milan

www.architettivalle.net
info@architettivalle.net
Tel +39 02 48013126

Index by architects

Index by project